The Busy Mom's Guide to Bible Study

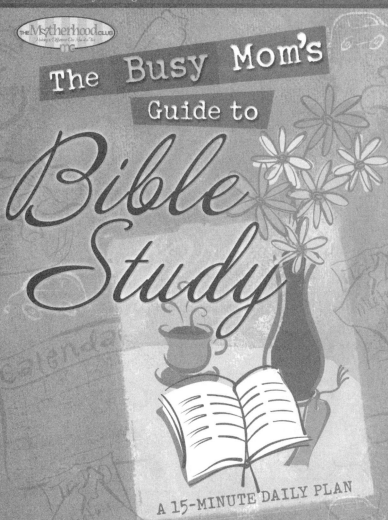

The Busy Mom's Guide to Bible Study

A 15-MINUTE DAILY PLAN

Lisa Whelchel

HOWARD BOOKS
A DIVISION OF SIMON & SCHUSTER, INC.
New York • Nashville • London • Toronto • Sydney

Howard Books, a Division of Simon & Schuster, Inc.
1230 Avenue of the Americas, New York, NY 10020

The Busy Mom's Guide to Prayer © 2005 by Lisa Whelchel
The Busy Mom's Guide to Bible Study © 2007 by Lisa Whelchel

First Howard Books trade paper edition April 2011

HOWARD and colophon are trademarks of Simon & Schuster, Inc.

For information about special discounts for bulk purchases, please contact Simon & Schuster Special Sales at 1-866-506-1949 or business@simonandschuster.com.

The Simon & Schuster Speakers Bureau can bring authors to your live event. For more information or to book an event, contact the Simon & Schuster Speakers Bureau at 1-866-248-3049 or visit our website at www.simonspeakers.com.

Manufactured in the United States of America

10 9 8 7 6 5 4 3 2 1

The Library of Congress has cataloged the original title as follows:

Whelchel, Lisa.
  The busy mom's guide to Bible study / Lisa Whelchel.
    p. cm.
  Summary: "Practical Bible study tools teach moms to have meaningful study time in just a few minutes a day"—Provided by publisher.
  Includes bibliographical references.
  1. Bible—Criticism, interpretation, etc. I. Title.
  BS511.3.W44 2007
  220.071—dc22   2007008978

ISBN 978-1-4516-4883-6

These titles were previously published individually.

*My heart is happy to dedicate this book to
three women I love and admire.*

It is a privilege to run alongside each of these sisters on this
journey to minister to women and lead them deeper in the
living, breathing, healing Word of God.

Beth Moore

You have led me into the very throne room of God and taught
me how to hear the Father's heartbeat and breathe deeply at
His feet. Your love for the Bible is contagious.

Priscilla Shirer

What an incredible friend you are to me, straight from the
Giver of every good and perfect gift, and that certainly defines
you! It is a joy to pray with you and play with you.

Angela Thomas

God has used you to expand my heart and to help me face my
fears, love with abandon, and acknowledge my need. I am
eternally grateful for my SBFF (Sweet Best Friend Forever).

*Say to wisdom, "You are my sister,"
and call insight your intimate friend.*

PROVERBS 7:4

Contents

Contents

Month 2

Contents

Month 3

Contents

Steve, Tucker, Haven, and Clancy – I know this book cost you a lot for me to write. I'm sorry I was away so much, not only physically, but also mentally and emotionally. Please forgive me, and thanks for your generous understanding. I know God will honor your sacrifice. I'm praying that when we get to heaven, there will be many moms who thank you personally.

Philis and Denny Boultinghouse – You have been above and beyond patient. Thank you for your gracious forbearance when I found myself with too many commitments clamoring for my attention at the same time. I know you love me first as a friend and then as an author.

Cyber Prayer Warriors – You carried my weary, stressed, overwhelmed heart before the Father for so many months. Just knowing you were praying gave me the confidence I needed on many days when I didn't think I was going to make it. I felt your love and support, and I am eternally grateful.

Scott Lindsey and Logos Bible Software – I can't imagine attempting to write this book without this amazing software and the tireless gift of your expertise. Thank you for providing the tool that has taken me deeper into the Word than I ever thought imaginable for a mom with barely a child-actress kind of education.

Morris Procter – I can't believe how much help you were able to give me in a handful of phone conversations. How do you know so much and keep it all at the top of your head and on

Acknowledgments

the tip of your tongue? You are a wealth of wisdom and a great friend to have, especially at a time like this.

Robert J. Morgan – What a privilege to work with you. Thank you for your humble response to my down-to-the-wire cry for help. You truly were a godsend.

Melanie Hill – I can always count on you! Thank you for being that kind of friend and a very present help in time of need. I love it that you enjoy doing what I don't want to do. And you're so good at it!

Al and Tracy Denson – I think you have been acknowledged in the last half dozen books I've written. I truly don't know what I would do without your generous hospitality to allow me to crash at your ranch to write for days on end. Your spiritual gift is definitely giving. I'm so thankful I get to be on the receiving end of your love for the Lord.

Ron Smith – We've been together through thick and thin. I love that about our partnership and friendship. Thank you for believing in me and representing my ministry with such passionate conviction.

I'm wondering why you picked up this book.

Are you like I am, wanting to go deeper in the Word and be more consistent with Bible study but so busy that you just end up feeling guilty about one more ball you've dropped in attempting to juggle so many? And then you feel guilty for even insinuating that time with God's Word would be something you merely juggle—much less drop!

Or maybe you've been fairly consistent with reading your Bible, but you'd like to take it to the next level: dig deeper and add a little more study to your Bible time.

I would love to think that some of you are reading these pages because we've become friends through some of my other books or my Web site. You know me personally and are confident that I will come alongside you, and together we'll discover how this whole Bible-study thing works in the life of a busy mom.

If you were given this guide or picked it up on your own but have no idea why, then you're in for a treat. I don't say that because I think I've written some phenomenal book. I dare to make such a statement because it sounds to me like God is wooing you—that He wants to reveal Himself to you in a deeper way through His Word. That's gotta feel good.

I wrote this book because I know both the challenge and the joy of digging deeper into God's Word. I've been reading my Bible daily since I was ten years old. At that time I was attend-

Introduction

ing a little Baptist church, and every Sunday morning I would place my coins in a tiny offering envelope, seal it, and check off the boxes: brought an offering, brought a friend, read my Bible. I desperately wanted to be a good little Christian girl.

In my teen years I discovered the privilege of intimacy that is possible by spending quiet time with Jesus every day, reading my Bible and praying. That all came to a screeching halt when I got married and had three babies in three years. I loved the idea of tarrying at the feet of Jesus for an hour each morning, but whenever I tried to get up before my children, I ended up just like the disciples: asleep. The spirit was willing, but the flesh wanted a nap.

Problem was, a nap couldn't satisfy my soul. As a mom, I love to give and give and give; but I wasn't receiving, and so I began to burn out. Even with three adorable children, a wonderful husband, and a gaggle of fun girlfriends, my heart longed for something more. Even in the middle of a room full of moms and kids, I often felt alone and empty.

What I needed was some warm, fresh Bread to fill me up. Jesus said, "I am the bread of life; whoever comes to me shall not hunger, and whoever believes in me shall never thirst" (John 6:35). He also said, "Man shall not live by bread alone, but by every word that comes from the mouth of God" (Matthew 4:4). I was hungry for Jesus, and His Word was the only nourishment that could sate my deepest cravings.

But I also desperately needed some guidance on how in the

world to raise these kids, bless my husband, get a semihot meal on the table, be a good friend, and reach out to my neighbor. I felt like I was failing miserably in every area. I needed help.

I asked my mother. I got on the phone with my friends. I read books written by marriage and parenting experts. I still felt like a failure.

Yet by being too busy and tired to spend time in God's Word, I was missing out on the best help available. Psalm 119:105 says, "Your word is a lamp to my feet and a light to my path." God promises to lead us and guide us, but we need His lamp and light to illuminate our way.

Still, the Bible is about more than guidance and direction; and by neglecting God's written Word, I was missing out on fellowship with God's Living Word, Jesus. He tells us, "If you abide in me, and my words abide in you, ask whatever you wish, and it will be done for you. By this my Father is glorified, that you bear much fruit and so prove to be my disciples" (John 15:7–8). Jesus also said, "No longer do I call you servants, for the servant does not know what his master is doing; but I have called you friends, for all that I have heard from my Father I have made known to you" (John 15:15).

Any friendship requires spending time together if it is to grow and thrive. Our friendship with God is no different, and the way we spend time with Him is through prayer—when we talk to God—and by spending time in His written Word—where He most often speaks to us. After all, what kind of friendships could we sustain if we only talked but never listened?

Introduction

I wanted that close relationship with Jesus, but I didn't understand how it could realistically fit in with all the demands of being a busy mom. I was still thinking of Bible reading as I had known it in the past: either a set amount of time that I spent daily in order to check it off the "Good Christian" list, or spending longer periods of time lingering in God's presence. For this season of my life, I needed to find some middle ground.

My attempts resulted in varying degrees of success. All I had ever known was a "more is more" mentality. I must read through my Bible in a year. Or spend an hour every morning. Or read five psalms and a Proverb daily. When I couldn't keep up, I would just give up.

Then I discovered a "Moore is more" approach. Someone introduced me to Beth Moore Bible studies. They offered structure and direction, and they were doable with a cup of coffee before the rest of the household woke up or while the kids were taking a nap or between the time I crawled into bed and when my husband turned off the news. I was in heaven.

After a while, though, I ran into a slight problem. I had worked through every one of her Bible studies and another dozen or so from other fabulous Bible teachers, and I realized I was becoming dependent on other people to study God's Word and then spoon-feed it to me.

Now, don't get me wrong. There is definitely a time and a place for packaged Bible studies, and if you haven't discovered these incredible resources, I highly recommend you rush to your

4

local Christian bookstore or do an Internet search and try some. But I knew God was calling me to go deeper into the cavernous dimensions of intimacy and relationship with Him.

I jumped in with excitement . . . only to discover that I was clueless on how to study the Bible for myself. I would open my Bible and stare at it for long periods of time, wondering where to start. Once I did start—basically just reading—I would look at my watch and realize the kids were going to get up any minute, so I'd better hurry up and pray. That was my version of Bible study on my own.

Some of my closest friends are seminary grads, which is a bit intimidating. Let me confess something right up front: I'm no expert on Bible study. All I know is that I am starving to know God, and I have searched for Him in His Word with desperate hunger. If you feel the same way, then come along with me, and we'll forage for Bread together.

I've never been to seminary, and much of what I'm sharing with you I have learned from the school of hard knocks—in this case meaning, I've been knocking really hard in accordance with Luke 11:9 ("Ask, and it will be given to you; seek, and you will find; knock, and it will be opened to you"). And God has been faithful to open up the Scriptures to me as I've asked Him to reveal Himself and sought Him diligently in His Word.

My goal is to encourage you that even as a busy mom, you can find more intimacy with Jesus than you ever thought possible. So often the focus is on quantity of Bible reading over

Introduction

quality of Bible study. We're going to change that perception as we work through this book together, and you'll find yourself going deeper in the Word in a shorter amount of time.

How to Use This Book

I'm going to share with you twenty fun Bible-study methods (or tools) that we will use together over the next three months. Five days a week (allowing a rest on Sunday and one "Yikes! I overslept!" day), we'll apply one of these tools to a fitting passage of Scripture. My desire is to show you, in a few pages per day, how to read one verse or short passage of Scripture and mine the gems hidden within by using these Bible-study techniques.

Month One

For the first month I'll be here holding your hand as we go, and by the end of the four weeks, you'll know how to apply twenty simple tools to find deep revelation in brief passages.

Each day of month one, in the Tools for Digging section I'll introduce and explain one Bible-study method. I've selected techniques that will be fun and simple to use. Most won't require any extra materials or resources, and you should be able to dig deep and uncover treasure in less than fifteen minutes a day.

Next, you'll read the Treasure Map, that day's scripture to be studied. It may be as long as a story or as short as a single verse. I've looked for passages that will be especially suited for laywomen like ourselves to study using our new tool.

Next in Going Deep, I'll model how to use our new study tool by sharing an example of how to apply the technique to the passage. This is just to be a good friend and jump into the deep end first so I can persuade you to plunge in too. If you have time, I encourage you to come on in—the water's fine. If you're not quite ready to get wet, you can wait to dive in next month, when we use these tools again.

The final page for each day, Discovery, will simply be blank lines. This is a place for you to record whatever insights the Holy Spirit quickens to your heart as you read the passage. Jot down any fresh perspectives the new Bible-study method reveals through my example. Or, if you're ready to give the new technique a try, this is the place to do it yourself.

Month Two

Our objective for the second month will be for me to let go of your hand but stay close enough to walk beside you. I may give a coaching tip here and there on the twenty new Bible-study methods we learned the previous month.

And this time, instead of repeating what we've already learned, I'll simply include a short list of bullet points on the first page to remind you of the main principles and applications. I will also include the page number on which that method was first introduced, in case you want a bit of refresher information.

The first page will also display a new passage of Scripture to study. Then it will be your turn to use the new Bible-study

Introduction

method to discover buried treasure for yourself. I may give a prompt to get you started, but the majority of the Going Deep page is full of blank lines so you can record what you've found and make notes on the process.

The last page for the day will be more of the guided-journal feature that is a key characteristic of every book in the Busy Mom's Guide series. This is where you can record your reflections on the day's digging and discovering.

Month Three

For the third and final month of our adventure together, it is my desire to see you begin walking this wondrous path on your own, while I stay just close enough to offer a bit of guidance along the way.

To accomplish this, on the first page I'll suggest three of the Bible-study methods we've learned, and you can select one to use for the day's passage, which is also on that page. On the next page you can make notes as you use one of the three recommended approaches to dig deep into God's Word. Then record the mysteries that were unlocked for you on the journaling page.

A New, Empowered You

I know in my heart that you will be a different woman at the end of these three months. That's the kind of power the Word of God has to transform lives. You'll find yourself responding more righteously, speaking with wisdom, and thinking Kingdom thoughts. This will happen without conscious effort, simply as a result of your drawing closer to Jesus, being strengthened in His presence, hiding the Word in your heart, and having your mind renewed.

My prayer is that, by the end of the three months, you'll feel confident that whenever you can find even ten minutes in the middle of your busy day, you can pick up your Bible, grab the study tool of your choice, and dig deep into a verse or short passage of Scripture. By doing so, you'll discover a beautiful treasure to display to your friends and family through a life changed by learning not just how to read your Bible but how to study it.

> *"If you seek it like silver*
> *and search for it as for hidden treasures,*
> *then you will understand the fear of the LORD*
> *and find the knowledge of God."*
>
> PROVERBS 2:4–5

Month 1

Tools for Digging

Asking the Five W's and an H

Who, *What*, *When*, *Where*, *Why*, and *How* are the "Five W's and
an H." These six interrogative words are considered fundamental
in journalism, police investigations, and research. The belief is
that if you can answer these six questions with facts, you'll have
the full story in a nutshell.

This is especially important in writing newspaper articles,
when journalists are limited in both time and space. (Sounds
like a busy mom's plight to me.) Police investigators must be able
to assess a crime scene quickly in order to cut to the chase and
solve the case. (Ever feel like that, Mom?) Researchers need a
simple grid along which to distill tons of information into practical help. (Mom again!)

These Five W's and an H are about to become your best
Bible-study friends. By reading a passage of Scripture and answering these six teeny-tiny, one-word questions, you can glean
loads of practical help, uncover beaucoup clues, and digest
hours' worth of information in a matter of minutes. Here's how
it works.

First, read a short passage or verse of Scripture.

Now, go back and ask yourself any or all of the famous W
and H questions. Eventually you'll come up with your own

specific five W's and an H questions, but these will get you started.

Who   Who is the main character? Who are the secondary characters? To whom is the main character talking? Referring?

What   What is the plot of this passage? What is happening? Is it a specific event?

When   When does the event or discourse in this passage occur (in history, in time, in chronology, in the character's life)? Don't rule out abstract time, such as "When the character realized he needed answers."

Where   Where did (or does or will) this event occur? Think about the setting, both broad and specific.

Why   Why is this happening? Why is this being said? Why did God include this passage in the Bible?

How   How did (or does or will) this happen? How did (or does or will) it affect the characters? Your life?

Treasure Map

On the way to Jerusalem he was passing along between Samaria and Galilee. And as he entered a village, he was met by ten lepers, who stood at a distance and lifted up their voices, saying, "Jesus, Master, have mercy on us." When he saw them he said to them, "Go and show yourselves to the priests." And as they went they were cleansed. Then one of them, when he saw that he was healed, turned back, praising God with a loud voice; and he fell on his face at Jesus's feet, giving him thanks. Now he was a Samaritan. Then Jesus answered, "Were not ten cleansed? Where are the nine? Was no one found to return and give praise to God except this foreigner?" And he said to him, "Rise and go your way; your faith has made you well."

LUKE **17:11–19**

Going Deep

Who—Jesus, the central figure, was met by ten leprous men as He passed through their area. Only one of the lepers, a Samaritan, proved to have a grateful heart.

What—The lepers, seeing Jesus, raised their voices and cried to Him for mercy. Jesus sent them to the local priest, who, according to Mosaic Law, could pronounce them whole. En route, their leprosy disappeared completely. They were healed before arriving at the priest's home. One of the men, the Samaritan, turned back and caught up with Jesus to give thanks.

When—This happened as Jesus was on His way to Jerusalem.

Where—The event took place on the border between Samaria and Galilee, at the outskirts of a village.

Why—It's not hard to imagine why the lepers wanted healing, but why did Jesus heal them? The key word is mercy. They cried, "Jesus, Master, have mercy on us." And the one leper who returned was motivated by gratitude. What a powerful attitude for me to take into the day—intense gratitude for God's immense mercy.

How—How did Jesus heal? With His powerful spoken word. How did the leper express His gratitude? He fell on his face at Jesus's feet, giving thanks to Him. The other nine lepers undoubtedly were excited about their restored health, but they didn't bother to express thanksgiving. How easy to take God's blessings for granted!

Discovery

(See instructions for use on page 7. These lines will be available to you at the end of each day's session.)

- Do not take God's blessings for granted.

- Always thank God for his mercy.

- God can make a change @ any time, always remember to thank Him.

Tools for Digging

Marking and Color Coding

Experts have identified three primary learning styles: visual, auditory, and kinesthetic. All this means is, each of us typically learns and remembers best either by seeing, hearing, or touching/experiencing. Identifying which way you receive and process information most effectively will be a tremendous help when studying your Bible and retaining what you've discovered.

The visual learner usually enjoys reading, is a fairly good speller, loves charts and diagrams, is stimulated by color, and needs peace and quiet to concentrate. Sound like you? Even if this isn't your primary learning style, using a different mode once in a while is good exercise for seeing things from another perspective.

To take advantage of a visual-learning strength, we're going to use marking and color-coding. Choose one or both options. Marking is probably the easiest. Just grab an ordinary pen or pencil. Then read your selected Bible verse or passage, marking any words that feel important to you. You can underline, circle, draw a box around, or star a word or phrase.

I always read a book with a pen in my hand. It helps me quickly reread the text to internalize the stuff I don't want to forget. I also end up writing little notes to myself in the margins. Your Bible may be set up with plenty of space to take notes or doodle—both things visual learners are prone to do. If it isn't, use a notebook.

Another great way to "see" the Bible is to collect a handful of various-colored highlighters (you can buy dry highlighters that won't soak through thin Bible pages) and create a color-coded system that means something to you. For instance, you may want to highlight every verse that has to do with the love of God in pink, faith in yellow, prayer in blue, promises in orange, and so forth.

If you keep up this technique, your Bible will be a virtual rainbow of markings. You'll be able to look at a verse or a passage and see both the big picture and the primary focus at a glance. This is just the kind of discovery that makes Bible study fun.

Blessed are the poor in spirit,
   for theirs is the kingdom of heaven.
Blessed are those who mourn,
   for they shall be comforted.
Blessed are the meek,
   for they shall inherit the earth.
Blessed are those who hunger and thirst
   for righteousness, for they shall be satisfied.
Blessed are the merciful,
   for they shall receive mercy.
Blessed are the pure in heart,
   for they shall see God.
Blessed are the peacemakers,
   for they shall be called sons of God.
Blessed are those who are persecuted
   for righteousness' sake, for theirs is
   the kingdom of heaven.

MATTHEW 5:3-10

Going Deep

I am grateful for my best friend Angela Thomas's insight on the Beatitudes. I wanted to highlight her refreshing perspective that this list of blessings isn't predicated on our needing to be all these things at one time in order to gain God's approval. Rather, *when we are* poor in spirit, *when we are* mourning, and so on, then the Kingdom of heaven will be established in our circumstances, we will be comforted, and so forth. To visually see the blessed promises, I chose to underline the condition and box the blessings.

Blessed are the poor in spirit, for theirs is the kingdom of heaven.

Blessed are those who mourn, for they shall be comforted.

Blessed are the meek, for they shall inherit the earth.

Blessed are those who hunger and thirst for righteousness, for they shall be satisfied.

Blessed are the merciful, for they shall receive mercy.

Blessed are the pure in heart, for they shall see God.

Blessed are the peacemakers, for they shall be called sons of God.

Blessed are those who are persecuted for righteousness' sake, for theirs is the kingdom of heaven.

MATTHEW 5:3–10

Discovery

Remember the blessings of
God. There is a blessing to
cover every circumstance

Day 3

Tools for Digging

Reading Aloud and Emphasizing
One Word at a Time

I thought I was a visual learner because I love to read and am obsessive about making charts. Then I researched the auditory learning style, and the first trait nailed me. Auditory learners typically love to hear the sound of their own voices. In other words, they talk a lot. Oops. They enjoy acting and being on stage. Who, me? They process ideas and information better by discussing them with friends, and they often love music. Let me pop in a CD, and let's talk about this.

It sounds to me like we can learn something from each of the learning styles. Even the fact that, without thinking about it, I used the word *sounds* in this sentence indicates an auditory learning style.

Auditory learners will learn twice as fast and retain information twice as long if they've heard it rather than just read it. That's one of the reasons simply reading the Bible is not always the best way to internalize God's Word. Auditory learners usually do this most effectively by reading the Bible aloud.

Today we're going to take this one step further. By reading the passage aloud and emphasizing one word at a time, we'll capitalize on not just one but two methods of going deeper in the Word and allowing it to seep into our souls.

Here's what I want you to do. Begin by reading the verse

aloud and loudly. Now read it aloud again, stressing the first word for meaning. Read it again, accentuating the second word. Again, emphasize the third word. Notice how every time you read the verse, concentrating on a different word, the verse takes on a deep meaning in its own unique way. Keep going until you've underscored each word in the scripture.

After you've completed this exercise, think back on which reading meant the most to you, and meditate on what God is saying to you through this revelation.

Treasure Map

> Delight yourself in the LORD, and he will give you the DESIRES of your heart.
>
> PSALM 37:4

Going Deep

Delight yourself in the LORD, and he will give you the desires of your heart.

Delight *yourself* in the LORD, and he will give you the desires of your heart.

Delight yourself *in* the LORD, and he will give you the desires of your heart.

Delight yourself in *the* LORD, and he will give you the desires of your heart.

Delight yourself in the *LORD*, and he will give you the desires of your heart.

Delight yourself in the LORD, *and* he will give you the desires of your heart.

Delight yourself in the LORD, and *he* will give you the desires of your heart.

Delight yourself in the LORD, and he *will* give you the desires of your heart.

Delight yourself in the LORD, and he will *give* you the desires of your heart.

Delight yourself in the LORD, and he will give *you* the desires of your heart.

Delight yourself in the LORD, and he will give you *the* desires of your heart.

Delight yourself in the LORD, and he will give you the *desires* of your heart.

Delight yourself in the LORD, and he will give you the desires *of* your heart.

Delight yourself in the LORD, and he will give you the desires of *your* heart.

Delight yourself in the LORD, and he will give you the desires of your *heart*.

PSALM 37:4

Discovery

When emphasized 1st word of sentence, "Delight" — able to focus on rest of sentence

Tools for Digging

Writing It Down and Walking It Out

Kinesthetic learners are a lot of fun! My son Tucker, like many people with ADHD, is a kinesthetic, or tactile, learner. He learns best by physically doing things. As his homeschool teacher, I've had to find and create a variety of hands-on learning experiences for this fun-loving boy.

Often kinesthetic learners are good at sports and process information best while moving rather than sitting around and thinking about it. (That would drive them absolutely bonkers—as well as everyone around them, since they'd probably be fidgeting the whole time they're supposed to be sitting still.)

If you're a tactile learner, I'll bet you enjoy "getting your hands dirty." You probably jump right in, tackling a problem before reading the instructions or seeking advice. You might say you learn best by experience. Maybe you have a short attention span and do better studying in short blocks of time. Sounds like you're holding the perfect book in your hand for this learning style!

If, as an experiential learner, you want to "taste and see" that the Lord is good, then have I got a great Bible study method for you! Like babies who put everything in their mouths to fully experience things, we're going to bite off one small chunk of

Scripture at a time and roll it around for a while to give God's Word plenty of time to be fully absorbed.

The first thing I want you to do is grab some flash cards. Just having something to hold in your hands is usually comforting to the tactile learner. Next, choose a passage or verse and write it out in longhand on your flash card. Never mind that kinesthetic learners tend to have messy handwriting—penmanship won't be graded, so don't sweat it. Typing may be good in everyday situations, but you won't receive the full benefit of this Bible-study method unless you actually write out the whole verse. Either cursive or printing will do. Studies show that handwriting is not just a motor process; it's also a memory process.

Then pull it all together by reading what you've written, as you walk around. I used to do this as an actress. I would often take my script and simply walk around the rehearsal hall reading my lines aloud. The combination of visual, auditory, and kinesthetic techniques shortened the time it took for me to memorize a new script each week. So as you walk and read your "lines" aloud, you are not only learning a new Bible-study skill today, but as a bonus, you will be hiding God's Word in your heart.

Treasure Map

Praise the Lord, all nations!
Extol him, all peoples!
For great is his steadfast love toward us,
and the faithfulness of the Lord
endures forever.
Praise the Lord!

PSALM 117

Going Deep

I chose Psalm 117 because I like the idea that I can write out a whole chapter of the Bible and walk it out—in every sense of the phrase—today. After grabbing a flash card from my Bible and writing out this chapter in my cursive that looks like a fourth grader's, I breathed a quick prayer asking God to help me internalize these verses as I studied them on the hoof, as it were. The first thing I noticed was that this chapter begins with a command, not just an inspirational suggestion: "Praise the Lord, all nations!" And by repeating the command, just changing the words around a bit ("Extol him, all peoples!"), God was emphasizing how strongly He felt about our making it a point to praise Him. And, not just you or I, or King David, or the children of Israel, but all nations—all peoples!

It isn't that God is on some kind of ego trip. As we look at the next verse, we see that we shouldn't need to be commanded; we have two of the best reasons to praise Him all day long spelled out for us right here. His steadfast love toward us is great, and His faithfulness is everlasting.

Then the psalm ends as it began, with the words "Praise the Lord!" My goal is to keep these two little verses in my pocket—and in my mind and heart—all day long, taking them with me into every situation I face. Like this psalm, I want to begin and end my day by praising the Lord.

Discovery

Begin + end our day praising the Lord

Tools for Digging

Praying the Scriptures

An immeasurable amount of anointing comes along with lining up our words with God's Word. It is alive. Hebrews 4:12 says, "The word of God is living and active, sharper than any two-edged sword, piercing to the division of soul and of spirit, of joints and of marrow, and discerning the thoughts and intentions of the heart."

I have a confession to make. I've never said this out loud before because I would really be embarrassed for someone to know. But sometimes if I'm reading a book and the author quotes a scripture, I skip over it because I've read it before. Isn't that terrible? I tell you this just in case you're ever tempted to do the same thing. Let's make a pact. From now on, when we find ourselves jumping ahead past the Scripture, we'll make it a point to go back and read it even more clearly. Start with the one I just quoted.

Can't you just feel the life and power? God created the whole world by His Word. Proverbs 18:21 says, "Death and life are in the power of the tongue." When we speak God's Word, we have the power to give life. When praying the Scriptures, I would even encourage you to speak aloud. After all, as we read in Genesis, God didn't just think about creation, "God *said* . . ." and there was life!

I've discovered that it's much easier for me to pray with faith when I can ground my requests in God's promises. He's given us hundreds of promises, but it's faith that unlocks them for us personally. Knowing that Hebrews 13:8 says, "Jesus Christ is the same yesterday and today and forever" and that if He did something in the Bible before, He can do it in my life today really bolsters my ability to believe and receive.

I also love to pray the psalms and the prayers in the Bible. Sometimes I don't even know exactly what I'm feeling, yet I'll flip open to the middle of the Book, and it seems the psalmist has read my mind and expressed my heart better than I could have done myself. Many times I'll read a passage aloud and put my name in it as many times as I can find a place to stick it in. Talk about making the Bible personal!

This morning, when I was digging around for my keys, an index card fell out of my purse. On it I had written out two of the prayers in the Bible that I wanted to claim, one for myself and the other for my children. Keeping these verses handy makes it easy for me to access the power of praying the Scriptures throughout the day.

Today I want you to read aloud the following passage and turn it into a prayer. Follow my lead, and I know you'll get the hang of it before next month.

Treasure Map

Be strong in the Lord and in the strength of his might. Put on the whole armor of God, that you may be able to stand against the schemes of the devil. For we do not wrestle against flesh and blood, but against the rulers, against the authorities, against the cosmic powers over this present darkness, against the spiritual forces of evil in the heavenly places. Therefore take up the whole armor of God, that you may be able to withstand in the evil day, and having done all, to stand firm. Stand therefore, having fastened on the belt of truth, and having put on the breastplate of righteousness, and, as shoes for your feet, having put on the readiness given by the gospel of peace. In all circumstances take up the shield of faith, with which you can extinguish all the flaming darts of the evil one; and take the helmet of salvation, and the sword of the Spirit, which is the word of God.

EPHESIANS 6:10–17

Going Deep

Lord, help me to be strong in You today, strong in the strength of Your might. I want to put on Your full armor so I can stand firm against Satan's schemes. I know that my struggle is not against flesh and blood but against the rulers and powers and dark forces of this world—and against the spiritual forces of wickedness in heavenly places. So with Your help I'm taking up the full armor of God so I can resist evil and stand firm. Help me put on the belt of truth, the breastplate of righteousness, and the shoes of readiness to share the gospel of peace. And above all, enable me to take up the shield of faith so I can extinguish all the flaming arrows the evil one shoots in my direction today. I want to wear the helmet of salvation and wield the sword of the Spirit—Your Word! Lord, may I be well armed, well dressed, and well defended today by Your power. In Jesus's name, amen.

Discovery

_____

_____

_____

_____

_____

_____

_____

_____

_____

_____

_____

_____

_____

_____

_____

_____

_____

Tools for Digging

Meditating on God's Word

The other night I couldn't sleep. My mind was racing. I was lying there, extremely busy planning, plotting, fixing, controlling, calendaring, writing, and worrying. After what felt like hours, I silently cried out, "Lord, please quiet my heart. I have to get some sleep." He answered with, "I will keep him in perfect peace whose mind is stayed on me, because he trusts in Me" (Isaiah 26:3, my paraphrase).

Of course, there was my answer. I immediately hopped out of bed, grabbed a stack of index cards, fired up my computer, squinted into the screen, and searched for about a dozen Scriptures I could keep handy to remind myself that my primary responsibility is to wait, rest, and trust. God will take care of everything; the *rest* is up to me.

I chose a verse I already had memorized and fell asleep meditating on that promise. The next morning when I awoke, the oppressive fog that had been clouding my vision for weeks had lifted. In place of darkness was the fresh light of revelation.

Meditation is a powerful tool for clearing your mind of things that distract from God and for setting your focus on things He approves.

My all-time favorite book is *Celebration of Discipline* by Richard J. Foster. Years ago, when I first read it and learned the importance of meditation, I thought he was referring to candles and incense and humming. Fortunately, it's a lot less esoteric than that. I read an article that helped me understand that "meditation is a combination of reviewing, repeating, reflecting, thinking, analyzing, feeling, and even enjoying."[1]

When you use this Bible-study method, I recommend beginning with a short passage, preferably one you've already committed to memory (or can memorize easily). Think about it all through the day and/or night. Psalm 1:2 says, "His delight is in the law of the LORD, and on his law he meditates day and night." The object is to focus on the nuance of each word, mull over each phrase, and let the whole verse linger in your heart and mind. Ask the Holy Spirit to give you a deeper revelation concerning a verse you've perhaps read a hundred times but always thought of in the same way until now. Let it come alive with manifold meaning.

Treasure Map

His delight is in the law of the Lord,
and on his law he meditates day and night.

He is like a tree
planted by streams of water
that yields its fruit in its season,
and its leaf does not wither.
In all that he does, he prospers.

PSALM 1:2–3

Going Deep

One thing I noticed while meditating on this verse was that the writer of this psalm actually demonstrated for us how he meditated on Scripture. I don't think it's too much of a stretch to think the writer may have been meditating on Joshua 1:8, where God commands us to keep reading and hearing His Word, thinking about it all day and night so that we might obey it. When we do, it promises, we will be prosperous and successful. Perhaps the writer was out in the sheep fields, near a tree-lined river, and noticed how fruitful and verdant the trees were, their roots irrigated by the flowing waters. I'm imagining that as David meditated on Joshua 1:8, he "rewrote" it in visual terms, likening Scripture meditators to the trees planted by streams of water, yielding fruit in the right season. Their leaves do not wither, and in whatever they do, they prosper.

As I learn God's Word and meditate on it day and night, I want to be like a fruitful tree and be prosperous in every way. I know that's possible because God's Word renews and redirects my mind so that I increasingly think as He does. Then I'll see things more clearly—from His perspective, through the lens of the Scripture passages I'm keeping fresh in my mind.

Discovery

Tools for Digging

Memorizing Scripture

I have Bibles all over the house, in my car, in my purse, and on my computer, PDA, and iPod. Even so, there are times when I'm caught somewhere without the Word handy. Thankfully, I have a bunch of it hidden in my heart so I'm never at a loss for "Words." There are many good reasons to memorize Scripture. I guess Psalm 119:11 is probably the biggest incentive: "I have stored up your word in my heart, that I might not sin against you."

Unfortunately, in my more honest moments, I sometimes get weary thinking about memorizing Scripture. I feel guilty enough about all the other important things I should be doing, and although the spirit is willing, my flesh is busy. Call it a mind game if you must, but one thing that has helped me is to think of this Bible-study method as Scripture repetition rather than Scripture memorization. I can certainly do the same thing over and over again. That is the life of a mom, isn't it?

Thankfully, this is the way we learn and memorize best anyway. Isaiah 28:10 puts it this way: "Precept upon precept, precept upon precept, line upon line, line upon line, here a little, there a little."

So here's what I want you to do today. Put a flash card on your car visor, or hang a little chalkboard in your kitchen, or stick a Post-it note at your desk, or make a Scripture screensaver.

Do whatever you need to do to keep the Bible verse you're memorizing—uh, I mean, repeating—in a place you will see it often. Then just read it again and again throughout the day. Don't forget to include the text reference. I always forget that part!

Another little trick that helps me is to draw a rudimentary picture as a cue to remember how the verse begins. Often I'm clueless when I see a text reference, but if someone will just prompt me with the first word, I can spout off the whole verse. For instance, I may write "Psalm 1:2" on the front of an index card, along with a little drawing of a lightbulb with the letter *D* in the middle.[2] This visually helps me remember that Psalm 1:2 says, "His delight (D-light) is in the law of the LORD, and on his law he meditates day and night."

Treasure Map

> I am the vine; you are the branches. Whoever abides in me
> and I in him, he it is that bears much fruit, for apart from
> me you can do nothing.
>
> JOHN 15:5

I liked memorizing this verse because it's simple, visual, and short. It also summarizes the entire fifteenth chapter of the gospel of John, which is one of my favorite soul-transforming, truth-packed chapters in the whole Bible. Here are some aids that helped me memorize it.

Remember that Jesus is speaking. In some Bibles the words of Jesus are printed in red type, so it helped me to visualize these words in red in my mind's eye. It also helped me to remember that this is one of Christ's seven famous "I am" statements recorded by John. "I am the vine." This may sound silly, but I drew a vine, with eyes in it, creeping all around the edges of my flash card. (Get it? Eye am the vine.) Then I drew a sheep to get me started on the next phrase, "Ewe [picture of a ewe] are the branches."

The rest of the verse contains a promise, and it helped me to see that the verse is divided up like this: a statement of fact ("I am the vine; you are the branches") followed by a promise ("Whoever abides in me and I in him, he it is that bears much fruit") followed by yet another fact—and what a fact it is ("apart from Me you can do nothing").

That's it. Fact-promise-fact. I love how by memorizing this one verse, we can absorb the truth of an entire chapter of the Bible and live it out at the same time.

Discovery

Tools for Digging

Reading from Parallel Translations

Do you have a favorite Bible translation? As a young believer I grew up reading from the King James Version, with all of its *thee*s and *thou*s. I was happy to discover the easier-to-read-and-understand paraphrase, the Living Bible, as a teenager. Today I enjoy reading from a handful of translations, but my current favorite is the English Standard Version (ESV).

You may think all Bibles are the same, but that isn't exactly the case. Some translations, like the ESV, New King James Version, and New American Standard Bible, are referred to as "essentially literal" translations. Basically, these are word-for-word translations from the original languages in which Scripture was recorded. Other translations—for example, the New International Version, the New Living Translation, and the Amplified Bible—are rendered thought for thought. These are also called "dynamic equivalent" translations. Some versions of the Bible aren't really translations at all. They would be better referred to as paraphrases. You may be familiar with some of these wonderful titles: the Message, the Living Bible, and the Good News Bible.

I believe there's merit in keeping on hand, and using, a variety of Bibles. I once spent a whole year reading the same chunk of Scripture out of a different Bible every day for a week at a time. I enjoyed beginning with a paraphrase to grasp the big picture and making my way to the King James Version with my Strong's Lexicon handy to help me get all the way back to the original-language definition.

Today we're going to explore the benefits of reading the same verse from a variety of translations and paraphrases. This being the first month of our walking this journey of Bible-study discovery together, I will provide these selections. But I encourage you to gather a small assortment of Bibles before next month, when you'll try this technique more on your own. You don't have to spend a lot or go to much trouble. It can be as simple as using your child's Bible, borrowing a friend's extra Bible, or visiting a Bible resource Web site such as BibleGateway.com.

This approach to Bible study is as simple as reading the same passage from a handful of translations and noticing how different words and concepts become richer by considering them from different perspectives.

Treasure Map

Do all things without grumbling or questioning, that you may be blameless and innocent, children of God without blemish in the midst of a crooked and twisted generation, among whom you shine as lights in the world.

PHILIPPIANS 2:14–15

Going Deep

The Message

Do everything readily and cheerfully—no bickering, no second-guessing allowed! Go out into the world uncorrupted, a breath of fresh air in this squalid and polluted society. Provide people with a glimpse of good living and of the living God. Carry the light-giving Message into the night.

New Century Version

Do everything without complaining or arguing. Then you will be innocent and without any wrong. You will be God's children without fault. But you are living with crooked and mean people all around you, among whom you shine like stars in the dark world.

New International Version

Do everything without complaining or arguing, so that you may become blameless and pure, children of God without fault in a crooked and depraved generation, in which you shine like stars in the universe.

The Amplified Bible

Do all things without grumbling and faultfinding and complaining [against God] and questioning and doubting [among yourselves], that you may show yourselves to be blameless and guiltless, innocent and uncontaminated, children of God without blemish (faultless, unrebukable) in the midst of a crooked and wicked generation [spiritually perverted and perverse], among whom you are seen as bright lights (stars or beacons shining out clearly) in the [dark] world.

Discovery

Tools for Digging

Looking for Rhema Rays

I've learned to take advantage of an abundance of resources to help this little wife-and-mother, Bible-teacher wannabe. One of my favorite go-to books is *Wuest's Word Studies from the Greek New Testament.* Since I can't read a bit of Greek (I will mercifully spare you the obvious "it's all Greek to me" joke), I turned to this resource to help me understand the definition of the word *logos,* which is most often translated "word" in the Bible. Here's what Wuest has to say: "The word is *Logos* (Λογος). It comes from the verb which means literally 'to pick out or select,' thus 'to pick words in order to express one's thoughts,' thus 'to speak.' It speaks of a word uttered by the human voice which embodies a conception or idea."[3]

Think about this with me for a minute. If you had an idea or abstract concept you were trying to articulate, what would be the easiest way to accomplish that? You would simply wrap words around your thoughts and express them, right?

When God, who is Spirit, wanted to communicate with us, He chose to do this by wrapping flesh around Spirit, thus embodying Himself to walk among us and express His nature: "The Word became flesh and dwelt among us, and we have seen his glory, glory as of the only Son from the Father, full of grace and truth" (John 1:14).

Another word often translated "word" in the Bible is the Greek transliteration *rhema*. Dr. Spiros Zodhiates, a recognized authority on the Greek New Testament, defines *rhema* as "sayings in particular as contrasted with sayings in their totality."[4]

Granted, *logos* and *rhema* are basically synonyms, like *big* and *large*. But the slight differences help me understand why sometimes a particular scripture will seem to leap off the page and straight into my spirit. While I sit in my recliner every morning, snuggled up with a cozy blanket, a cup of hot coffee, and my favorite Bible, on some days, as I'm reading the Word to know God personally, He reveals Himself in an especially intimate way. It's as though God shines a ray of light on a verse, and even if I've read it a hundred times before, suddenly I understand how it specifically applies to me and my life. I call these moments "rhema rays."

Today I want you to pray a specific prayer before you turn to the "Treasure Map." Ask the Holy Spirit to ignite a particular verse or phrase within the passage, shining a rhema ray straight into your heart.

Treasure Map

He who dwells in the shelter of the Most High
    will abide in the shadow of the Almighty.
I will say to the Lord, "My refuge and my fortress,
    my God, in whom I trust."
For he will deliver you from the snare of the fowler
    and from the deadly pestilence.
He will cover you with his pinions,
    and under his wings you will find refuge;
    his faithfulness is a shield and buckler.
Because you have made the Lord your dwelling place—
    the Most High, who is my refuge—
    no evil shall be allowed to befall you,
    no plague come near your tent.
For he will command his angels concerning you
    to guard you in all your ways.

PSALM 91:1–4, 9–11

Going Deep

Maybe it's because I'm a mom, but the rhema ray for me in this passage is in verse 10, "no plague come near your tent." My peace and happiness is so tied to my family that for me to feel the full impact of peace and assurance packed in this passage, I need to hear that my household will be protected.

I often realize that my own mistakes and weaknesses cause collateral damage to my children. When I think of plagues, my mind immediately goes to punishment for rebellion or sin. I don't want my shortcomings to cost my family. In order to prevent that, I must run to the Lord and live in Him, trusting Him to cover those I love. I have to depend on Him to defend us and keep the enemy at bay. Only He can absorb the punishment for my sin in His righteousness and grant salvation to me and my household. So I will ask Him to guard me and keep me in all my ways.

Discovery

Tools for Digging

Using a Dictionary

Over the next six days I'm going to introduce you to a bookshelf full of invaluable resources for Bible study. Now, here's my dilemma: one of my primary goals for this book is to help you see that you can have meaningful times of studying God's Word in the midst of a mom's crazy schedule. Yet some of the more fun Bible-study methods might require a bit more time than you have available in your day. And a few of them are greatly enhanced by resources that you may not have lying around the house. So we're going to have to figure out a way to get access to the resources (so we can get the good stuff from the Bible-study method) without stressing you out in the process.

Actually, accessing the resources is the easiest part. You can do this by logging on to a Bible-resource site on the Internet, doing a search on the Web, taking advantage of the many wonderful Bible-software programs, or, last but not least, using the age-old, tried-and-true sources: books. To help you, I've compiled a list of specific Web sites, software, books, and other resource recommendations. You can find these in the appendix to this book on page 236.

If you don't have Internet access in your home or you can't afford Bible software, or if the idea of hauling your kids to the library or bookstore leaves you with a less-than-enthusiastic attitude toward pursuing quality Bible-study time, don't lose heart. I'll include some easier modifications for each new Bible-study method I introduce.

Today we'll choose an easy but extremely beneficial resource: a simple dictionary. Many words we read in the Bible are not used in our modern vernacular—words like *propitiation*, *sanctification*, *redemption*, and *atonement*. We may think we know what these words mean, but I've discovered that I always learn something new by looking up the word in one of my kids' school dictionaries.

If you want to go a step further, try to get a Webster's 1828 dictionary. Because it used the King James Version as its base for definitions, this dictionary defines words from that era. It helps define words as they were understood a few centuries ago, when the KJV was first published.

So go dig in your child's backpack, look on the bookshelf or in the junk drawer, or try one of the many online dictionaries. Then grab your Bible in anticipation of a mini English lesson!

Treasure Map

The righteousness of God has been manifested apart from the law, although the Law and the Prophets bear witness to it—the righteousness of God through faith in Jesus Christ for all who believe. For there is no distinction: for all have sinned and fall short of the glory of God, and are justified by his grace as a gift, through the redemption that is in Christ Jesus.

ROMANS 3:21–24

59

Looking the key terms up in Merriam-Webster's online dictionary, here's what I found:

- *Righteous*—acting in accord with divine law; free from guilt or sin; morally right or justifiable.

- *God*—the supreme or ultimate reality; the Being perfect in power, wisdom and goodness who is worshipped as creator and ruler of the universe.

- *Manifest*—to make evident or certain by showing or displaying.

- *Faith*—belief and trust in and loyalty to God; complete trust.

- *Believe*—to have a firm conviction as to the goodness, efficacy, or ability of something; to consider to be true or honest.

- *Sin*—an offense against religious or moral law; transgression of the law of God.

- *Glory*—praise, honor; something that secures praise or renown; a distinguished quality or asset.

- *Justify*—to prove or show to be just, right, or reasonable; to qualify, judge, regard, or treat as righteous and worthy of salvation.

- *Grace*—favor, unmerited divine assistance; virtue coming from God; disposition to kindness or clemency.

- *Redeem*—to buy back; repurchase; to get or win back; to free from what distresses or harms.[5]

The overall theme that jumped out at me after reading these definitions was that God is the initiator and force behind our salvation. It has nothing to do with what we do; it's all about His free gift, favor, and power!

Discovery

_____

_____

_____

_____

_____

_____

_____

_____

_____

_____

_____

_____

_____

_____

_____

_____

_____

_____

Tools for Digging

Choosing a Topical Study

One of my favorite ways to dig into the Bible is to choose a topical study. Sometimes I want to know more about a particular subject, such as grace or prayer or forgiveness. By thoroughly researching a topic, we can get a bigger picture of what God wants to convey through His Word than if we only look at snapshots—isolated verses here or there—now and then.

Other times I desperately need to hear what God has to say on a matter, such as temptation or money—or children! Too often, when I'm struggling through a confusing time, I'll call a friend or look for a book on the subject, all the while overlooking the best Friend and greatest Book available. There is no greater resource combo we can turn to when trying to figure out how to make life work.

Many helpful resources are available to make launching into a topical study simple and engaging, but today we're going to focus on using a concordance. The most readily available concordance is more than likely in the back of your Bible, probably near the maps. Online concordances are easy to find too, but I recommend purchasing an exhaustive concordance to keep near your Bible and journal.

An exhaustive concordance will tell you every single time a word occurs in the Bible. If you really want to get fancy, look in a Strong's or New American Standard Bible concordance. These books will also tell you the original Hebrew, Greek, or Aramaic word used in each instance. (We'll talk more about mining biblical treasures in the original languages in a few days.)

After you've chosen your topic, simply look up that word in your concordance. Most of the time the word will be shown within the context of the sentence in which it appears. This makes it easier to narrow your search—especially handy if you're trying to accomplish a search in one sitting, as we are today. Just look up as many references as time allows.

One idea you might want to pay attention to is the "law of first mention." The basic concept is that the first time a word is mentioned in the Bible is exceptionally important and sets the tone and standard for the way it's interpreted in subsequent appearances. Just a little extra incentive not to skip over the first listing!

Well, alrighty then. Let's go.

Go your way. Eat the fat and drink sweet wine and send portions to anyone who has nothing ready, for this day is holy to our Lord. And do not be grieved, for the joy of the LORD is your strength.

NEHEMIAH **8:10**

Going Deep

Nehemiah 8:10 tells us that the Lord's joy in our lives boosts our morale, fuels our enthusiasm, and gives us energy for daily living—the joy of the Lord is our strength. So what else does the Bible say about joy? Looking up this little three-letter, one-syllable word in the Bible unlocks a world of . . . well, joy. A check of the concordance shows that this word occurs 179 times in the English Standard Version of the Bible. I looked up a few examples from the book of Psalms: 4:7; 5:11; 16:11; 20:5; 30:5; 51:12; 66:1; and 119:111.

Just from these eight references, I learned that I should experience more joy than those who have "hit the jackpot" in this world, for believers have a God-given joy. When we find our refuge in Him, we'll have a continual song of joy in our lives, for joy comes from living in God's presence and trusting in His Word. We find joy not only in our salvation but in God's answers to our prayers—even though our joy may be preceded by periods of weeping. And if we've somehow lost our joy, not to worry: God is able to restore it to us.

Tools for Digging

Exploring Different Perspectives

If I could recommend only one additional Bible-study resource to invest in, it would definitely be the Logos Bible Software program. (No, I don't get any remuneration for recommending their product. I simply love it and want to tell everyone about it.) But if you'll need to wait and save up money for that one, my next suggestion would be a good study Bible. Fortunately, there are so many to choose from, you won't have any trouble finding something that fits your needs.

My favorite is the *Spirit-Filled Life Bible*, edited by my former pastor, Jack Hayford. Some of my friends recommend *The MacArthur Study Bible*, edited by John MacArthur. Think of having these resources like having Jack Hayford or John MacArthur sitting in your living room as you study, sharing their insights on what a certain passage of Scripture means.

A study Bible is an excellent choice for your daily devotions because you can go in-depth while studying even a short passage, which is exactly what I've been trying to help you do these last two weeks. One of the most helpful features of a study Bible is the introductory information or overview provided at the beginning of each new book of the Bible. This section explains when that book was written, who wrote it, the cultural context, and the overall theme of the book. Some also alert you to key verses to watch for.

Study Bibles are similar to commentaries in that they contain other people's opinions and interpretations of the Scriptures; they are simply tools to be used in addition to the Bible itself. The main thing to keep in mind is that any commentary is written by a fallible person, and his or her interpretation of Scripture is subjective. Even so, I have thoroughly enjoyed the commentaries I've owned over the years, and I find them especially helpful when I encounter a passage that's difficult to understand. The perspectives offered in these resources help me get over the hump to better understanding.

I'm just naturally the kind of person who is interested in others' views. Sure, I can toss out their ideas if they don't resonate with what the Spirit of God is speaking to me; but nine times out of ten, hearing from someone else broadens my perspective and deepens my understanding.

And if you can't find a study Bible or commentary, then a really good alternative might be to call a friend and ask her to read today's Treasure Map passage and call you back with what she got out of it. Chances are she'll have discovered something you overlooked. How fun is that?

Jesus answered them, "Go and tell John what you hear and see: the blind receive their sight and the lame walk, lepers are cleansed and the deaf hear, and the dead are raised up, and the poor have good news preached to them. And blessed is the one who is not offended by me."

MATTHEW 11:4–6

My main question upon reading this passage was, What does that last sentence mean? "Blessed is the one who is not offended by me." I checked a handful of commentaries, and this is what I discovered:

- Blessed is he who, in spite of all hindrances, shall find himself able to believe in Me as the Messiah.[6]

- They are blessed because they take no offense at Jesus, accepting him as the promised Messiah. Many Jews, however, did take offense at Jesus. Some versions say "cause to stumble," referring to Jews "stumbling" over Jesus because he did not meet their political and nationalistic messianic expectations, even though Jesus's words and deeds were worthy of the Messiah. So Jesus warned John and all the Jews not to allow their expectations to drive a wedge between them.[7]

- In beatitude form Jesus encourages John, and everyone else with similar doubts, to remain faithful to him no matter what may come. "Fall away" (offended) is from the key Matthean term *skandalizō*, which in various contexts can be translated "take offense, stumble, or cause to sin" and is cognate to our English *scandalize*.[8]

- Blessed is the one who is not upset by the way I run my business.[9]

One way these commentaries shed light and offered a fresh perspective on this verse was in reminding me that John didn't have the New Testament; but he knew the Law and the Prophets inside and out. Without the benefit of hindsight, the children of Israel were taught to look for a king, a ruler, or a governor as the Messiah. Jesus didn't seem to fit the bill, and it was confusing and conflicting to this good Jewish boy.

Discovery

Tools for Digging

Studying Historical Contexts

I love the Bible, and I love history, so you can imagine how excited I am to share with you today's Bible-study method. Let's first talk about the resources available for studying the historical and cultural context for some of our favorite passages. The most general would be a Bible handbook. This handy little volume is part Bible dictionary with some commentary added to the mix; throw in some archaeological facts and church history, add a dash of manners and customs for seasoning, sprinkle with some really helpful pictures and illustrations. Sound like a must-have to you?

A Bible dictionary or Bible encyclopedia is similar but much more exhausting . . . uh, I mean exhaustive. This is the place to go if you're a true-blue history buff or detail person. You will be in Bible-study heaven.

A manners-and-customs book makes for some fun reading all by itself. It's fascinating to learn about how people lived during Bible times—the clothes they wore, jobs they had, food they ate, or just how they went about their daily lives and how different from, and yet similar to, our own everyday existence they were.

Let me share a few instances in which you would enjoy reaching for one of these resources (or even a regular, do-they-even-publish-them-anymore encyclopedia). Let's start with a doozy, 1 Corinthians 11:2–16, where Paul says it's disgraceful for a woman to have short hair and how she needs to be wearing a head covering anyway. I like Paul, but sometimes he can rub me the wrong way. This would be one of those times. Thankfully, I was able to cut Paul a little slack after researching first-century Corinth and discovering why he was even bringing up this issue in light of the dress custom, society's view on hair issues, and women in general. A quick peek into one of these handy resources reveals that short hair or a shaven head marked one as a prostitute or a loose woman.

You can also look at single verses, such as Matthew 5:13 ("You are the salt of the earth, but if salt has lost its taste, how shall its saltiness be restored? It is no longer good for anything except to be thrown out and trampled under people's feet"). This verse takes on a whole new depth of meaning in light of how salt was used in Bible times. Since salt was used for preservation as well as for flavoring, we learn that Christians are to have a profound influence on society—an influence that makes a lasting difference.

I've chosen a really fun verse for us to study today. Come join me.

Follow me, and I will make you fishers of men.

MATTHEW 4:19

Going Deep

When I think of fishing, I visualize a pole, a line, and a hook with a squirmy, gooshy worm on the end. I imagine casting the line out on the lake, waiting for a tug, and reeling in the fish. So when I read this verse about being catchers of men, that's what I think I should do in my personal evangelism. How important history and culture and customs are to the study of the Bible!

By looking up some history on fishing in Bible times, I learned that fish were most often caught in a dragnet, which was shaped like a long wall, with sinkers along one side and cork on the opposite side. The net is positioned in a large semicircle some distance from the shore, then slowly pulled to land by two teams of eight fishermen each. The work was often done at night, when the fish couldn't see the cords of the nets and swim away.

I learned so much through this little bit of investigation that my thinking was transformed. For one thing, this information seems to indicate that we should work in teams to spread the gospel. Perhaps evangelism was never meant to be done alone, or to be completely dependent on individuals. Just as Paul illustrated with different imagery in 1 Corinthians 3, one person plants, the other waters, and the Holy Spirit brings the increase. Fishing is a team sport.

Tools for Digging

"Interviewing" through Biographical Study

A biographical study is one of most fascinating methods of Bible study, but it can also be a bit time consuming, so here's what we're going to do. I am going to share with you some foundational tools for digging up information on a character in the Bible. You can either choose to learn about a lesser-known character more quickly, or you can explore a more prominent person over the course of many days. Your choice.

The first order of business is choosing someone to study. Think of a Bible character who reminds you of yourself. Are you more like Peter or Paul or Mary? You can learn a lot about this person and yourself at the same time by studying him or her. Or perhaps you want to choose a character you know relatively nothing about and would like to know more. Don't rule out the bad guys. Much wisdom can be gained by studying how *not* to live like a king in the Old Testament.

A great resource to get started studying Bible characters is a cross-reference. Hopefully, in your Bible you will notice tiny numbers next to some of the words in the text. Look at the bottom of the page, or sometimes in a center column, for the corresponding number. There you will find a reference to another biblical text. Follow that trail to, perhaps, another tiny number that will lead you to yet another verse.

If you're really getting into this treasure hunt, you may want to access one of two incredible books. *The Treasury of Scripture Knowledge* is a huge cross-reference volume that is versified, or organized, just like your personal study Bible. But it is Sasquatch compared to the little footnotes in your Bible. It includes a cross-reference for each and every verse in the whole Bible! You could be gone for days following all those trails and jumping from verse to verse. But think of the great adventure you would have and all you'd discover along the way.

Now, for a biographical sketch, I've found no better tool than *Nave's Topical Bible*. I love this resource because the cross-references are organized by topics and even subtopics. Let me warn you: you might not want to start with a major personality like Paul or David. These entries list so many verses, it'll make your head swim.

Just think. By the end of your "interview," you'll feel like you know that Bible character on a personal level. Can you imagine how this will transform your reading every time you encounter him or her in the Bible from now on?

Treasure Map

I am reminded of your sincere faith, a faith that dwelt first in your grandmother Lois and your mother Eunice and now, I am sure, dwells in you as well.

2 TIMOTHY 1:5

I liked learning about Eunice because she's a character who can be easily studied, and although she doesn't appear many times in the Bible, the lessons from her life translate personally to me as a mother. Here are some of the cross-references I found and what I learned from them:

- *2 Timothy 1:5.* This verse reveals several things about this biblical mother. She possessed a sincere faith in Jesus Christ, as did her own mother, Lois. These two women were responsible for raising a man who would become one of the first and finest pastors in Christian history—Timothy, who penned two letters included in the New Testament.

- *2 Timothy 3:14–15.* Eunice taught her son Timothy the Word of God from the time he was an infant.

- *Acts 16:1–5.* We're told that Eunice was Jewish and that she was a believer who was married to a Greek man, evidently not a Christian. Their son Timothy had embraced the faith of his mother and grandmother, and the Christians in that area spoke well of him.

By compiling the passages about Eunice, I not only better understand the books of 1 and 2 Timothy, but I gain a composite model for myself as I endeavor to be a godly mother and, eventually, grandmother.

Discovery

Tools for Digging

Investigating Original Languages

Don't let the idea of ancient languages scare you. Trust me, you don't have to be fluent in a foreign language, or even know how to speak pig Latin. We can gain an amazing depth of insight into the Bible just by learning a few basics.

The Old Testament was originally written primarily in Hebrew, because it is the history of the children of Israel, and that's the language they spoke. The New Testament was written primarily in the Koine, or street, Greek, because it was the language of the day. Getting His Word into the hands of everyday people would make the most sense for why God would choose common Greek as the Good News language. (Some Aramaic is sprinkled throughout the Bible too, but for today let's just keep things simple.)

In the early fifth century A.D., the Bible was translated into Latin. But it wasn't until the sixteenth century, after the Protestant Reformation, that English translations were made. OK, history lesson over. Let's learn why this is important to us now.

As with any transition from one language to another, whether from Hebrew to Greek, or Greek to Latin, or Hebrew to English, something is always lost in translation. To complicate things even further, often multiple words in the original language are translated into only one English word. For instance, in the Psalms, David is always telling us to praise the Lord; but David used a variety of distinct Hebrew words that all ended up being translated into our one English word *praise*. It's sad, really, because so much texture and color gets lost or becomes bland when forced into the confines of the English language. So it's important that we know which Hebrew or Greek word our English word represents in order to uncover its vibrant meaning.

Today we're going to learn how to use word-study dictionaries, like *Strong's Exhaustive* (KJV), *NAS Exhaustive*, or *The Strongest NIV Exhaustive* concordances. These resources list the words used in our English Bible along with the Greek or Hebrew words and meanings, and they are invaluable in helping us get back to the original intended message of God's Word.

It's a lot easier than you'd think to do a miniexegesis. Here are the simple, pseudoseminary steps.

First, read the passage and choose a key word. Look up that word in one of the above-mentioned concordances. (Don't forget, these resources are also available online or via Bible software.) In the entries under that word, find the reference to the text you're reading. A Strong's or GK number will be listed to the right of your verse—jot this down. Now go to the back of your concordance, where you'll find a sort of dictionary called a lexicon. Find your number, and there you'll see the Hebrew or Greek word that was originally used, along with multiple definitions. Voilà! You've just used the original languages to mine the deeper truths of Scripture.

We all, with unveiled face, beholding the glory of the Lord, are being transformed into the same image from one degree of glory to another. For this comes from the Lord who is the Spirit.

2 CORINTHIANS 3:18

Going Deep

This verse is one of the greatest in the Bible on the topic of Christian growth. As rich as the verse is in the English, it sparkles even more when we peek at a couple of the original words Paul used as he wrote in Koine Greek.

- *Behold*—κατοπτρίζομαι (katoptrizomai)—The Greek here could have one of two meanings, which accounts for differences between translations. One meaning is "to see, behold, or contemplate," and the other is "to reflect." We must study this verse to see whether it's telling us to behold the beauty of Christ or to reflect it. The ESV chooses *behold*, but the NIV translators use the word *reflect*.

- *Transformed*—μεταμορφόομαι (metamorphoomai)—Look at that Greek term carefully. Does it remind you of an English term? Yep—metamorphosis, which means a change in form, such as a caterpillar becoming a butterfly. This is one of the New Testament's most unexpected and glorious terms. In Romans 12:2 we're told that we should not be conformed to this world but be transformed by the renewing of our minds.

By looking up the original words, this verse became much more powerful to me. I learned that by gazing at the glory of God, in the mirror image of Christ, I am literally changed from one degree of glory to another by the Holy Spirit. I will never be the same again!

Month 1
Day 15 *Discovery*

Tools for Digging

Using Your Imagination

We need to use our imagination more as adults. We should daydream more often. We need to remember the words of Jesus in Mark 10:15: *Whoever does not receive the kingdom of God like a child shall not enter it.* How often do you get really still and let your mind wander, allowing your ears to perk up to hear the still, small voice that cannot be heard above the other small-but-not-so-still voices saying, "Mommy, Mommy, Mommy" a hundred times a day?

We've already had our seminary lesson for the month; today it's time for kindergarten. Albert Einstein had it right when he said, *Logic will take you from A to B. Imagination will take you everywhere.* I want you to think of one of your favorite passages from the Bible. Now, close your eyes. (Keep your hands to yourself, no touching your neighbor on the mat beside you!) Imagine yourself in the middle of that Bible scene. Ask as many questions as you can think of in order to really convince yourself you've been transported back to Bible times.

Okay, I'm going to stop for one minute and address anyone who is getting a little freaked out, wondering if I've gone New Age or something. Imagination and creativity are wonderful, God-given gifts. Who can blame the world for trying to steal them? But however the enemy distorts them, they were ours as children of the Creator first, so let's get over our paranoia and get back to daydreaming before it's snack time.

Are your eyes closed? Silly question, I know—just checking to make sure you're still with me. OK, in your mind's eye, look all around. Don't forget to look behind you too. What do you see? Is it summer or winter? Are a lot of people around, or just a handful? What do you hear? Locusts? Children squealing? Can you smell anything, like bread baking or stinky disciples per-haps? What about taste? Sea salt in the air? Dust? If there's food, take a bite of it. What about your sense of touch? Reach out and grab hold of something near you. Are you hot and sweaty? Gritty dirty?

How do you feel emotionally? Anxious? excited? in love? tired? What are you thinking about? *What am I doing here? Will He notice me?* What happened just before this Bible passage be-gan? Where are you going to go next? What is the person saying in this verse? How would you respond if you were right there, right now? Start up a conversation with the people in the pas-sage. What would you ask them? Do they answer? What do they say?

Stick around as long as you like. When you're ready to leave, we'll try this exercise together with the Treasure Map verse.

Treasure Map

"O our God, will you not execute judgment on them? For we are powerless against this great horde that is coming against us. We do not know what to do, but our eyes are on you."

Meanwhile all Judah stood before the LORD, with their little ones, their wives, and their children. And the Spirit of the LORD came upon Jahaziel the son of Zechariah, son of Benaiah, son of Jeiel, son of Mattaniah, a Levite of the sons of Asaph, in the midst of the assembly. And he said, "Listen, all Judah and inhabitants of Jerusalem and King Jehoshaphat: Thus says the LORD to you, 'Do not be afraid and do not be dismayed at this great horde, for the battle is not yours but God's. Tomorrow go down against them. Behold, they will come up by the ascent of Ziz. You will find them at the end of the valley, east of the wilderness of Jeruel. You will not need to fight in this battle. Stand firm, hold your position, and see the salvation of the LORD on your behalf, O Judah and Jerusalem.' Do not be afraid and do not be dismayed. Tomorrow go out against them, and the LORD will be with you."

Then Jehoshaphat bowed his head with his face to the ground, and all Judah and the inhabitants of Jerusalem fell down before the LORD, worshiping the LORD.

2 CHRONICLES 20:12–18

As I travel back in time in my imagination, I land in the middle of a city gripped by fear. I have lived in Jerusalem and enjoyed peace for years, but suddenly comes the dramatic news that enemy armies are en route; in fact, they're only a day's march away. I can smell the fear as the whole population gathers in the city center, knowing that within a day their families could be massacred. Normal activities cease. The world comes to a standstill.

I put myself in the king's shoes. With no army equal to the challenge, I feel utterly helpless. At first I'm alarmed, but then I determine to seek God's help. I assemble the people. Even without microphone or amplifier, my trembling voice is audible because no sound arises except, perhaps, the desert wind. It is as still as death. I pray, "We do not know what to do, but our eyes are on you."

The "amen" is sounded by all, but not a soul moves. Not a baby whimpers. Not a dog barks. Suddenly a cry arises from Jahaziel as the Spirit of God comes over him, and he utters this message: "Do not be afraid and do not be dismayed at this great horde, for the battle is not yours but God's."

I don't think I would have slept that night. It would have been the longest, darkest hour of my life as I looked at the sleeping forms of my children in their beds. Would they be brutally killed the next day, or could I trust God to keep His promise?

When I read the story as if I were there, I have to ask myself if I would have trusted the Lord and sung His praise at such a time as that. I don't know. But it's a powerful reminder to face my everyday battles with the power of praise.

Discovery

_____

_____

_____

_____

_____

_____

_____

_____

_____

_____

_____

_____

_____

_____

_____

_____

_____

_____

_____

Tools for Digging

Summarizing for the Big Picture

Because I'm a bottom-line kind of person, I love this Bible study method. My husband, Steve, on the other hand, loves details. When new friends come over to our house for dinner and want a tour, I stand in the middle of the hall and point to the kids' rooms upstairs, the master bedroom at the end of the hall, and the kitchen and family room around the corner. Then I make sure they know where the guest bathroom and the laundry room are located. The bathroom for obvious reasons; the laundry room because that's where I've usually thrown everything before they arrived, and I definitely don't want them opening that door.

On the other hand, if I'm running late getting dinner on the table, I'll ask Steve to give our guests the grand tour. This guarantees me at least another half hour to make up for the time I spent cleaning the house (i.e., throwing all the junk into the laundry room), since he'll go into great detail describing the wiring in the guest-bedroom closet.

Obviously, there's a time and a place for both personality types. In the same way, there's a time to dissect each and every word in a passage of Scripture, and there's also great benefit in seeing how few words you can use to internalize or express the writer's thoughts.

When we summarize a story, passage, or chapter from the

Bible, we're concentrating on distilling the main thoughts, central theme, or big ideas from the text. This gets really fun after a while, when we can put all of our little summaries together and see the big picture of an entire book of the Bible.

So the first thing I want you to do is read today's passage through at least five times, aloud if possible. Don't think too hard, just read the story, enjoy it, and get the overall gist of it. Did you notice any repeated words? How about a central lesson, verse, or theme? What happened at the beginning, in the middle, and at the end?

Read it one last time. Now, give the passage a title. Then break it down into natural divisions, and try to summarize each section in one sentence. Wrap it up with one last summary statement of the overall theme. And there you have the bottom line.

One day he got into a boat with his disciples, and he said to them, "Let us go across to the other side of the lake." So they set out, and as they sailed he fell asleep. And a windstorm came down on the lake, and they were filling with water and were in danger. And they went and woke him, saying, "Master, Master, we are perishing!" And he awoke and rebuked the wind and the raging waves, and they ceased, and there was a calm. He said to them, "Where is your faith?" And they were afraid, and they marveled, saying to one another, "Who then is this, that he commands even winds and water, and they obey him?"

LUKE 8:22–25

Going Deep

This is one of my favorite stories—Jesus calming the storm. It's so short that I read through it in about half a minute, but I was able to summarize it further by reading it several times and boiling it down to its essential lessons.

The first thing that helped was noticing that there are three clear scenes in this story: before, during, and after the storm. I also took note of the repetition of the word *Master*. I felt like the key phrase of the story was in verse 25: "Where is your faith?" Here's my summary of this paragraph and its lesson.

Jesus was weary from doing His Father's work, and He fell asleep in the boat. He was so confident of His Father's care that He kept right on sleeping in the midst of a raging storm. His disciples were tired too, but less trusting. Jesus, awakened, rebuked the winds; but He also rebuked His disciples with the simple question, "Where is your faith?" It's the same question He asks me when I give in to fear, which needs to be replaced with faith and trust in the Lord. He is all-powerful, and He has everything under control—even when I sometimes feel He's asleep at the keel.

Month 1
Day 17 *Discovery*

96

Tools for Digging

Paraphrasing to Assimilate Truth

Paraphrasing, or expressing someone else's ideas in your own words, is a great Bible-study method because it forces us to internalize the passage enough to make it our own. Interestingly, a paraphrase is a form of literature that was birthed in the church. Before the Protestant Reformation in the sixteenth century, the Bible was only available in the Latin Vulgate version. But evangelists and missionaries needed to be able to share God's Word in a language the townspeople could understand. And so the first paraphrases of the Bible, or any work of literature for that matter, were produced. Cool, huh?

In my own life, I've paraphrased passages for a variety of reasons. To share a difficult truth with a seeking friend. To personalize a promise from God's Word. To contemporize biblical concepts for my children in more accessible language. But mostly, just as a fun exercise to help me assimilate God's truth and let it seep into every pore of my being.

The first step in paraphrasing is to read the passage several times—a couple of times just to get the overall idea and then a few more times, paying closer attention to details. If you don't understand some portion, resist the urge to conjecture or simply guess based on the context. The trick to paraphrasing is changing the words without changing the meaning.

Think about paraphrasing as if you were giving directions to someone. You're sharing information from your point of view, which is fine, but if you leave out anything or add a turn here or there, that person will probably get lost—even though you were only trying to help, and you mostly knew how to get to the destination . . . sort of.

After reading through the passage multiple times, think about how you would share its truth with a friend. You can do this with the passage as a whole, or you can break it down line by line—whatever feels best to you. Pay close attention to antiquated words, or phrases that reflect a culture from days gone by. What would be a more modern way of expressing the same idea?

Hopefully, when you've finished, you'll be able to express God's truth in a way even a teenager would understand. (I didn't say a child because, in my experience, teens are more difficult to convince that wisdom from thousands of years ago can still apply to their lives in practical and appealing ways.) Paraphrasing is a great language with which to communicate with the generation—adolescent or adult—of today.

Treasure Map

Rejoice in the Lord always; again I will say, Rejoice. Let your reasonableness be known to everyone. The Lord is at hand; do not be anxious about anything, but in everything by prayer and supplication with thanksgiving let your requests be made known to God. And the peace of God, which surpasses all understanding, will guard your hearts and your minds in Christ Jesus.

Finally, brothers, whatever is true, whatever is honorable, whatever is just, whatever is pure, whatever is lovely, whatever is commendable, if there is any excellence, if there is anything worthy of praise, think about these things. What you have learned and received and heard and seen in me—practice these things, and the God of peace will be with you.

PHILIPPIANS 4:4–9

Here's what to do when you're worried: make up your mind to be joyful, and let your joy be based on your relationship with Christ. I'll say that again: rejoice in the Lord! Treat others with gentleness, and let everyone see your patience in action. Remember, you have the Lord as near you as your very hand. So don't cave in to anxiety; instead, turn your worries into prayers, praying about every single thing that concerns you. And let your prayers be earnest pleas laced with genuine thanksgiving. That's the way to experience the peace of God, which transcends all our needs, wants, desires, fears, feelings, and expectations. His peace will protect your heart and mind, guarding you against despair. That's why it's important to focus your thoughts on what is true, honorable, right, pure, lovely, exemplary, excellent, and praiseworthy. Meditate on such things, and the God of peace Himself will be with you.

Discovery

Tools for Digging

Teaching Your Children

One of the best ways to learn something is to teach it to someone else. The benefits of this Bible-study method are similar to the ones we develop through paraphrasing, in which we must understand and internalize the information before we can put it into our own words. Teaching the passage takes this one step further. We have to figure out how to convey the material in a way that is not just understandable but also engaging and worthy of attention. And we moms have the perfect guinea pigs: our children.

I've been homeschooling my children for more than twelve years. I have a gifted child, an excellent student, and a wild man. You'd think I would need to teach in three different ways, but the truth is, the principles I'm going to share with you today work no matter how old your children are or how much they enjoy, or don't enjoy, learning.

The first thing to remember is that teaching should be as interactive as possible. That does not mean simply filling your child's head with knowledge about the Bible. It means sharing ideas and soliciting questions and feedback all along the way. This will keep your kids engaged—and you'll have to stay on your toes and really know the material to stay one step ahead of them, which helps *you* learn more.

Give your children a reason to want to listen. Ask yourself, from their point of view, "Why? Who cares? So what?" Can you make it worth their while? Of course you can—it is the Word of God you're teaching.

Choose a parable or story to teach. Moms instinctively know that stories are the language of children. If you can, use pictures. Children retain 70 percent more with visuals. Or you may want to let them draw a picture themselves. This will keep them occupied and, believe it or not, help them focus on your story better. Incorporate as many senses as possible. Hey, serve popcorn or chocolate-chip cookies during your "class." They'll certainly never forget you, their favorite teacher ever.

As I mentioned earlier in the book, we learn best by repetition; but that doesn't mean by redundancy. Repeat the message, but say it in a different way, or tell it from a different perspective to really drive home a key point in the passage.

Be sure to engage your kids' emotions, and make it fun. Insert something ridiculous and see if they catch it. It will grab their attention and make them remember the truth you were acting silly about. Pause every once in a while and have each child tell you what they've just heard, or if they're older, ask them to tell you the story.

The bonus that comes with this method of studying the Bible is that your children learn a Bible passage too. The goal is that you learned even more by teaching it.

Love is patient and kind; love does not envy or boast; it is not arrogant or rude. It does not insist on its own way; it is not irritable or resentful; it does not rejoice at wrongdoing, but rejoices with the truth. Love bears all things, believes all things, hopes all things, endures all things.

1 Corinthians 13:4–7

Going Deep

This simple passage about the world's most popular theme—love—lists fifteen qualities of genuine, God-given love. In teaching this passage to our children, the goal is to transfer the qualities of love from the printed page to our kids' hearts. Here are some ideas, exercises, techniques, and tips you can try. Choose one or two, and enjoy some edutainment with your child.

- Make flash cards, each listing one of the fifteen traits, and help your child assemble them in order according to the biblical text.

- Ask your kids if they have any friends or teachers who are rude and impatient or if they know anyone who fits the description in this passage. Sometimes identifying what the opposite quality looks like helps us zero in on the goal.

- Try making a song from one of the verses in this passage. All of us, with a little effort, can compose a simple tune for, say, verse 4.

- Have each child read the passage, substituting his or her name for the word *love*. Love is an abstract concept, but it suddenly takes on flesh when we learn to say, "I am patient. I am kind. I am not jealous. I don't brag, and I'm not arrogant." While none of us practices perfect love all the time, this is the pattern Christ wants to develop within us.

- Teach your children to turn this passage into a prayer. ("Lord, help me to be patient and kind . . .")

- Discuss how Jesus perfectly exemplifies all of these qualities and how these fifteen traits describe the way He treats us.

Tools for Digging

Making Practical Application

> Don't just listen to God's word. You must do what it
> says. Otherwise, you are only fooling yourselves. For if
> you listen to the word and don't obey, it is like glancing
> at your face in a mirror. You see yourself, walk away, and
> forget what you look like. But if you look carefully into
> the perfect law that sets you free, and if you do what
> it says and don't forget what you heard, then God will
> bless you for doing it.
>
> JAMES 1:22–25 NLT

We've covered a lot of ground in the past month, but the last
thing I want is for you to learn twenty Bible-study methods, dig
deep into the Word, and come up with a bunch of head knowledge but no heart change. We must be careful, as 1 Corinthians 8:1–2 reminds us: "'Knowledge' puffs up, but love builds up.
If anyone imagines that he knows something, he does not yet
know as he ought to know."

God gave us His Word not merely to inform our minds but
primarily to change our lives. We don't want to simply know a lot
of Scripture and yet have our lives remain unchanged, so we must
learn what it means to be a doer of the Word. How do we put

our faith into action? James 2:18 says, "Show me your faith apart from your works, and I will show you my faith by my works."

Although this is just one of twenty tools for Bible study we've discussed, it's one I suggest trying to incorporate every day, in addition to whatever other method you're using at the moment. Each time we read God's Word, our response should be, "Lord, what do You want me to do with this information? How can I apply this principle to my life, starting today? Am I violating this scripture in word, thought, or deed?"

Get into the habit of spending the last few minutes of your quiet time actually being quiet. This is a struggle for me. I feel like I should be praying or worshipping or writing in my journal or reading my Bible; being still and quiet seems like a waste of time. That's how I feel. Yet I know that it's crucial to be still enough to hear the Holy Spirit speak to us about how He wants us to respond to what we've learned in the Word.

Of course, we don't want to miss the obvious. If the passage tells us to do something or not to do something, we don't need to ask the Holy Spirit for further revelation—we need to just do it (unless it says not to)! But we may need to take a minute to ask the Holy Spirit to help us "just do it."

Let's try this practical-application method together and see how we can take the wonderful truths we've been learning and use them to help us live out a life of truth.

You have no excuse, O man, every one of you who judges. For in passing judgment on another you condemn yourself, because you, the judge, practice the very same things. We know that the judgment of God rightly falls on those who do such things. . . .

All who have sinned without the law will also perish without the law, and all who have sinned under the law will be judged by the law. For it is not the hearers of the law who are righteous before God, but the doers of the law who will be justified.

ROMANS 2:1-2; 12–13

When I read this passage, I was sorely convicted about a certain situation. A person in my life had hurt me deeply. I knew in my heart that I had forgiven this person and was able to move on in the relationship without bitterness. I thought I had responded righteously and that everything was settled and behind me. But God used this verse to show me that while I had forgiven this individual for hurting me, I still needed to repent for judging the person. For one thing, I was capable of doing the same thing, and I certainly would want mercy to be extended toward me. The best way to guarantee that is to live not only in forgiveness but also by passing out mercy instead of judgment.

Every passage of Scripture has a lesson for us, and we grow deep in the faith as we make our own Bible translations—not from Greek to English but from the printed pages to our daily lives. Bible study without personal application is like reading the label of a medicine bottle without ever taking the medicine to cure your illness. It's like perusing cookbooks without ever preparing a meal or carrying a canteen through the desert without ever sipping the water. For it is not the hearers of the Word who are righteous before God; it is the doers of the Word who will be justified.

May God help us to . . . just do it!

Discovery

_____

_____

_____

_____

_____

_____

_____

_____

_____

_____

_____

_____

_____

_____

_____

_____

_____

_____

_____

Month 2

Tools for Digging

Asking the Five W's and an H

(To review, see page 12.)

Who?
What?
When?
Where?
Why?
How?

Eli the priest was sitting on the seat beside the doorpost of the temple of the LORD. [Hannah] was deeply distressed and prayed to the LORD and wept bitterly. And she vowed a vow and said, "O LORD of hosts, if you will indeed look on the affliction of your servant and remember me and not forget your servant, but will give to your servant a son, then I will give him to the LORD all the days of his life, and no razor shall touch his head."

Eli observed her mouth. Hannah was speaking in her heart; only her lips moved, and her voice was not heard. Therefore Eli took her to be a drunken woman. And Eli said to her, "How long will you go on being drunk?" But Hannah answered, "No, my lord, I am a woman troubled in spirit. I have drunk neither wine nor strong drink, but I have been pouring out my soul before the LORD. I have been speaking out of my great anxiety and vexation." Then Eli answered, "Go in peace, and the God of Israel grant your petition that you have made to him." And she said, "Let your servant find favor in your eyes." Then the woman went her way and ate, and her face was no longer sad.

1 SAMUEL 1:9–18

Going Deep

Who is the main character?_____

_____

What is happening? _____

_____

When does the event or discourse in this passage occur? _____

_____

Where did (or does or will) this event occur?_____

_____

Why was this being said? _____

_____

How did (or does or will) it affect the characters? _____

_____

Discovery

_____

_____

_____

_____

Tools for Digging

Tools for Digging

Marking and Color Coding

(To review, see page 17.)

- Circle, star, or box key words.
- Take notes in the margins.
- Highlight themes with a variety of colors.

Treasure Map

> Oh sing to the Lord a new song;
>> sing to the Lord, all the earth!
> Sing to the Lord, bless his name;
>> tell of his salvation from day to day.
> Declare his glory among the nations,
>> his marvelous works among all the peoples!
> For great is the Lord, and greatly to be praised;
>> he is to be feared above all gods.
> For all the gods of the peoples are worthless idols,
>> but the Lord made the heavens.
> Splendor and majesty are before him;
>> strength and beauty are in his sanctuary.
>
> PSALM 96:1–6

Going Deep

Write down Psalm 96:1–6 and highlight or underline the various attributes of God in this passage. Then record your response to them.

_____

_____

_____

_____

_____

_____

_____

_____

_____

_____

_____

_____

_____

Discovery

Tools for Digging

**Reading Aloud and Emphasizing
One Word at a Time**

(To review, see page 22.)

- *Read* the verse aloud and loudly.
- *Speak* the verse multiple times.
- *Emphasize* the first word, then the second, third, etc.

Treasure Map

> Seek first the kingdom of God and his
> righteousness, and all these things will be added
> to you.
>
> MATTHEW 6:33

Going Deep

Now write Matthew 6:33, emphasizing a different word each time you write the verse (see page 25 for an example).

_____

_____

_____

_____

_____

_____

_____

_____

_____

_____

_____

_____

_____

_____

_____

Discovery

_____

_____

_____

_____

_____

_____

_____

_____

_____

_____

_____

_____

_____

_____

_____

_____

_____

_____

Tools for Digging

Writing It Down and Walking It Out

(To review, see page 27.)

- Get flash cards.
- Write in longhand.
- Walk around while reading aloud.

Treasure Map

> You keep him in perfect peace
>> whose mind is stayed on you,
>> because he trusts in you.
> Trust in the Lord forever,
>> for the Lord God is an everlasting rock.
>
> ISAIAH 26:3–4

Going Deep

_____

_____

_____

_____

_____

_____

_____

_____

_____

_____

_____

_____

_____

_____

_____

_____

_____

Discovery

Tools for Digging

Praying the Scriptures

(To review, see page 32.)

- *Personalize* the scripture with your name.
- *Change* pronouns to reflect your prayer.
- *Claim* promises for your life.

For this reason I bow my knees before the Father, from whom every family in heaven and on earth is named, that according to the riches of his glory he may grant you to be strengthened with power through his Spirit in your inner being, so that Christ may dwell in your hearts through faith—that you, being rooted and grounded in love, may have strength to comprehend with all the saints what is the breadth and length and height and depth, and to know the love of Christ that surpasses knowledge, that you may be filled with all the fullness of God.

Now to him who is able to do far more abundantly than all that we ask or think, according to the power at work within us, to him be glory in the church and in Christ Jesus throughout all generations, forever and ever. Amen.

EPHESIANS 3:14–21

Going Deep

Discovery

Tools for Digging

Meditating on God's Word

(To review, see page 37.)

- Read aloud or think about the verse all day or night.
- Isolate each word and concentrate on its meaning.
- Ask the Holy Spirit for deeper revelation.

Treasure Map

> "I am the Alpha and the Omega," says the Lord God, "who is and who was and who is to come, the Almighty."
>
> REVELATION 1:8

Going Deep

Discovery

Tools for Digging

Memorizing Scripture

(To review, see page 42.)

- Write the verse on a flash card.
- Illustrate the first word prompt.
- Put in a prominent place.
- Read it often throughout the day.

Treasure Map

Enter by the narrow gate. For the gate is wide and the way is easy that leads to destruction, and those who enter by it are many. For the gate is narrow and the way is hard that leads to life, and those who find it are few.

MATTHEW 7:13–14

Going Deep

_____

_____

_____

_____

_____

_____

_____

_____

_____

_____

_____

_____

_____

_____

Discovery

_____
_____
_____
_____
_____
_____
_____
_____
_____
_____
_____
_____
_____
_____
_____
_____
_____

Tools for Digging
Reading from Parallel Translations

(To review, see page 47.)
- Gather a variety of Bibles.
- Read the same passage in each translation.
- Notice differences.

Treasure Map

If, in our endeavor to be justified in Christ, we too were found to be sinners, is Christ then a servant of sin? Certainly not! For if I rebuild what I tore down, I prove myself to be a transgressor. For through the law I died to the law, so that I might live to God. I have been crucified with Christ. It is no longer I who live, but Christ who lives in me. And the life I now live in the flesh I live by faith in the Son of God, who loved me and gave himself for me. I do not nullify the grace of God, for if justification were through the law, then Christ died for no purpose.

GALATIANS 2:17–21

Going Deep

Discovery

Tools for Digging

Looking for Rhema Rays

(To review, see page 52.)

- Pray.
- Ask the Holy Spirit to speak to you.
- Read.
- Listen.

Treasure Map

What then shall we say to these things? If God is for us, who can be against us? He who did not spare his own Son but gave him up for us all, how will he not also with him graciously give us all things? Who shall bring any charge against God's elect? It is God who justifies. Who is to condemn? Christ Jesus is the one who died—more than that, who was raised—who is at the right hand of God, who indeed is interceding for us. Who shall separate us from the love of Christ? Shall tribulation, or distress, or persecution, or famine, or nakedness, or danger, or sword? As it is written,

"For your sake we are being killed all the day long; we are regarded as sheep to be slaughtered."

No, in all these things we are more than conquerors through him who loved us. For I am sure that neither death nor life, nor angels nor rulers, nor things present nor things to come, nor powers, nor height nor depth, nor anything else in all creation, will be able to separate us from the love of God in Christ Jesus our Lord.

ROMANS 8:31–39

Going Deep

"Dear Lord, please open the eyes of my heart to see treasures You've hidden just for me. Let me hear You in practical, personal ways about things concerning me and areas You want to highlight in my life. Thank You for speaking to me through Your Word."

_____

_____

_____

_____

_____

Discovery

_____

_____

_____

_____

_____

_____

Tools for Digging

Using a Dictionary

(To review, see page 57.)

- Find a dictionary.
- Look up key words.
- Reflect on their deeper meanings.

Treasure Map

> If anyone is in Christ, he is a new creation. The old has passed away; behold, the new has come. All this is from God, who through Christ reconciled us to himself and gave us the ministry of reconciliation; that is, in Christ God was reconciling the world to himself, not counting their trespasses against them, and entrusting to us the message of reconciliation. Therefore, we are ambassadors for Christ, God making his appeal through us. We implore you on behalf of Christ, be reconciled to God. For our sake he made him to be sin who knew no sin, so that in him we might become the righteousness of God.
>
> 2 CORINTHIANS 5:17–21

Month 2
Day 10 *Going Deep*

You may choose to look up the words *reconciliation, trespasses, entrusting, ambassadors,* and/or *righteousness.*

_____

_____

_____

_____

_____

_____

_____

_____

_____

_____

_____

_____

_____

_____

_____

_____

_____

Discovery

_____

_____

_____

_____

_____

_____

_____

_____

_____

_____

_____

_____

_____

_____

_____

_____

_____

_____

_____

Tools for Digging

Choosing a Topical Study

(To review, see page 62.)

- Look up the topic in a concordance.
- Go to a handful of the listed references.
- What is the overall message?

Treasure Map

Bring the full tithes into the storehouse, that there may be food in my house. And thereby put me to the test, says the LORD of hosts, if I will not open the windows of heaven for you and pour down for you a blessing until there is no more need.

MALACHI 3:10

Going Deep

Look up the word *tithe* in a concordance.

_____

_____

_____

_____

_____

_____

_____

_____

_____

_____

_____

_____

_____

_____

Tools for Digging

Exploring Different Perspectives

(To review, see page 67.)

- Read notes for this verse in a study Bible.
- Look up the reference in a commentary.
- Share insights with a friend.

Treasure Map

He is the radiance of the glory of God and the exact imprint of his nature, and he upholds the universe by the word of his power. After making purification for sins, he sat down at the right hand of the Majesty on high.

HEBREWS 1:3

Month 2
Day 12 *Going Deep*

_____

_____

_____

_____

_____

_____

_____

_____

_____

_____

_____

_____

_____

_____

_____

_____

Discovery

Day 13

Tools for Digging

Studying Historical Contexts

(To review, see page 72.)

- Find an encyclopedia, Bible dictionary, or Bible handbook.
- Look up historical and cultural content.
- Read the passage again with new (or would that be old?) eyes.

Treasure Map

Jesus answered them, "Destroy this temple, and in three days I will raise it up." The Jews then said, "It has taken forty-six years to build this temple, and will you raise it up in three days?"

JOHN 2:19–20

Going Deep

Find historical information on Solomon's temple.

_____

_____

_____

_____

_____

_____

_____

_____

_____

_____

_____

_____

_____

_____

_____

_____

_____

_____

_____

Month 2
Day 13 *Discovery*

_____
_____
_____
_____
_____
_____
_____
_____
_____
_____
_____
_____
_____
_____
_____
_____
_____
_____
_____
_____

Tools for Digging Day 14

"Interviewing" through Biographical Study

(To review, see page 77.)

- Choose a person(s) to study. (I've chosen Aquila and Priscilla for you.)
- Look up today's verse and see if any cross-references are listed.
- Look online or in a cross-reference book for related scriptures.
- Follow them to gain a composite picture of your chosen Bible character.

Treasure Map

> He found a Jew named Aquila, a native of Pontus, recently come from Italy with his wife Priscilla, because Claudius had commanded all the Jews to leave Rome. And he went to see them.
>
> ACTS 18:2

Find verses that mention Aquila and Priscilla or Claudius.

_____
_____
_____
_____
_____
_____
_____
_____
_____
_____
_____
_____
_____
_____
_____

Discovery

_____

_____

_____

_____

_____

_____

_____

_____

_____

_____

_____

_____

_____

_____

_____

_____

_____

_____

_____

Day 15 · *Tools for Digging*

Investigating Original Languages

(To review, see page 82.)

- Choose key word(s) to define.
- Look up the word in a concordance.
- Find Strong's number beside the verse reference.
- Go to the lexicon in the back of the book and find that number.

Treasure Map

When they had finished breakfast, Jesus said to Simon Peter, "Simon, son of John, do you love me more than these?" He said to him, "Yes, Lord; you know that I love you." He said to him, "Feed my lambs." He said to him a second time, "Simon, son of John, do you love me?" He said to him, "Yes, Lord; you know that I love you." He said to him, "Tend my sheep." He said to him the third time, "Simon, son of John, do you love me?" Peter was grieved because he said to him the third time, "Do you love me?" and he said to him, "Lord, you know everything; you know that I love you." Jesus said to him, "Feed my sheep."

JOHN 21:15–17

Look up the word *love* each time it is used in this passage, and note the different meanings.

_____

_____

_____

_____

_____

_____

_____

_____

_____

_____

_____

_____

_____

_____

Tools for Digging

Using Your Imagination

(To review, see page 87.)

- Close your eyes and grow still.
- Imagine yourself in the setting of the passage.
- Give attention to each of your senses.
- Ask as many questions as you can think of.

Treasure Map

He went in to his father and said, "My father." And he said, "Here I am. Who are you, my son?" Jacob said to his father, "I am Esau your firstborn. I have done as you told me; now sit up and eat of my game, that your soul may bless me." But Isaac said to his son, "How is it that you have found it so quickly, my son?" He answered, "Because the LORD your God granted me success." Then Isaac said to Jacob, "Please come near, that I may feel you, my son, to know whether you are really my son Esau or not." So Jacob went near to Isaac his father, who felt him and said, "The voice is Jacob's voice, but the hands are the hands of Esau." And he did not recognize him, because his hands were hairy like his brother Esau's hands. So he blessed him. He said, "Are you really my son Esau?" He answered, "I am." Then he said, "Bring it near to me, that I may eat of my son's game and bless you." So he brought it near to him, and he ate; and he brought him wine, and he drank.

Then his father Isaac said to him, "Come near and kiss me, my son." So he came near and kissed him. And Isaac smelled the smell of his garments and blessed him and said,

"See, the smell of my son is as the smell of a field that the LORD has blessed!"

GENESIS 27:18–27

Going Deep

_____

_____

_____

_____

_____

_____

_____

Discovery

_____

_____

_____

_____

_____

_____

Day 17 | Tools for Digging

Summarizing for the Big Picture

(To review, see page 92.)

- Read the passage at least five times.
- Give it a title.
- Divide sections into one-sentence themes.
- Write a summary statement.

Treasure Map

[Jesus] entered the temple and began to drive out those who sold and those who bought in the temple, and he overturned the tables of the money-changers and the seats of those who sold pigeons. And he would not allow anyone to carry anything through the temple. And he was teaching them and saying to them, "Is it not written, 'My house shall be called a house of prayer for all the nations'? But you have made it a den of robbers." And the chief priests and the scribes heard it and were seeking a way to destroy him, for they feared him, because all the crowd was astonished at his teaching.

MARK 11:15–19

Going Deep

Tools for Digging

Paraphrasing to Assimilate Truth

(To review, see page 97.)

- Read the passage several times.
- How would you share it conversationally?
- Rephrase any antiquated words.

Treasure Map

Do not be deceived: God is not mocked, for whatever one sows, that will he also reap. For the one who sows to his own flesh will from the flesh reap corruption, but the one who sows to the Spirit will from the Spirit reap eternal life. And let us not grow weary of doing good, for in due season we will reap, if we do not give up. So then, as we have opportunity, let us do good to everyone, and especially to those who are of the household of faith.

GALATIANS 6:7–10

Going Deep

_____

_____

_____

_____

_____

_____

_____

_____

_____

_____

_____

_____

_____

_____

_____

_____

_____

_____

_____

_____

_____

Discovery

Day 19 | Tools for Digging

Teaching Your Children

(To review, see page 102.)

- Read the passage several times.
- Paraphrase it.
- Ask yourself why your child would want to learn this.
- Incorporate the senses.
- Use repetition.
- Engage emotion.

Treasure Map

Like cold water to a thirsty soul,
    so is good news from a far country.
Like a muddied spring or a polluted fountain
    is a righteous man who gives way before the wicked.
It is not good to eat much honey,
    nor is it glorious to seek one's own glory.
A man without self-control
    is like a city broken into and left without walls.

PROVERBS 25:25–28

Going Deep

You may want to gather a few of the following supplies to make this passage come alive for your children: a glass of ice-cold water, water with dirt in it, a jar of honey and a big spoon, and a LEGO building set to build a fortress and tear down a wall.

_____

_____

_____

_____

_____

_____

_____

_____

_____

_____

_____

_____

_____

_____

Discovery

Tools for Digging

Making Practical Application

(To review, see page 107.)

- Be quiet and still.
- Ask the Holy Spirit to examine your heart and life.
- Think of a way to live out this verse.

Have unity of mind, sympathy, brotherly love, a tender heart, and a humble mind. Do not repay evil for evil or reviling for reviling, but on the contrary, bless, for to this you were called, that you may obtain a blessing. For

"Whoever desires to love life
and see good days,
let him keep his tongue from evil
and his lips from speaking deceit;
let him turn away from evil and do good;
let him seek peace and pursue it.
For the eyes of the Lord are on the righteous,
and his ears are open to their prayer.
But the face of the Lord is against those who do evil."

1 Peter 3:8–12

Going Deep

"Dear Lord, I bring my heart before You, submitting it to the Light of Your Son. I yield my life to the gentle probing of the Holy Spirit. Show me how I can live out these Words of Yours in a practical way today."

_____

_____

_____

_____

_____

_____

Discovery

_____

_____

_____

_____

_____

_____

Month 3

Tools for Digging

Tool Suggestions

- Investigating Original Languages
- Making Practical Application
- Writing It Down and Walking It Out

Treasure Map

Do not love the world or the things in the world. If anyone loves the world, the love of the Father is not in him. For all that is in the world—the desires of the flesh and the desires of the eyes and pride in possessions—is not from the Father but is from the world. And the world is passing away along with its desires, but whoever does the will of God abides forever.

1 John 2:15–17

Going Deep

_____

_____

_____

_____

_____

_____

_____

_____

_____

_____

_____

_____

_____

_____

_____

Discovery

Tools for Digging

Tool Suggestions

- Reading Aloud and Emphasizing One Word at a Time
- Choosing a Topical Study
- Using a Dictionary

Treasure Map

> Jesus said to him, "I am the way, and the truth, and the life. No one comes to the Father except through me."
>
> JOHN 14:6

Going Deep

Discovery

Tools for Digging

Tool Suggestions

- Marking and Color Coding
- Meditating on God's Word
- Looking for Rhema Rays

Treasure Map

> Even youths shall faint and be weary,
>   and young men shall fall exhausted;
> but they who wait for the Lord shall renew
>   their strength;
>   they shall mount up with wings like eagles;
> they shall run and not be weary;
>   they shall walk and not faint.
>
> ISAIAH 40:30–31

Going Deep

Discovery

Tools for Digging

Tool Suggestions

- Asking the Five W's and an H
- Using Your Imagination
- "Interviewing" through Biographical Study

Treasure Map

After [Abram's] return from the defeat of Chedorlaomer and the kings who were with him, the king of Sodom went out to meet him at the Valley of Shaveh (that is, the King's Valley). And Melchizedek king of Salem brought out bread and wine. (He was priest of God Most High.) And he blessed him and said,

"Blessed be Abram by God Most High,
Possessor of heaven and earth;
and blessed be God Most High,
who has delivered your enemies into your hand!"

And Abram gave him a tenth of everything. And the king of Sodom said to Abram, "Give me the persons, but take the goods for yourself." But Abram said to the king of Sodom, "I have lifted my hand to the LORD, God Most High, Possessor of heaven and earth, that I would not take a thread or a sandal strap or anything that is yours, lest you should say, 'I have made Abram rich.' I will take nothing but what the young men have eaten, and the share of the men who went with me. Let Aner, Eshcol, and Mamre take their share."

GENESIS 14:17–24

Going Deep

_____

_____

_____

_____

_____

_____

Discovery

_____

_____

_____

_____

_____

_____

Tools for Digging

Tool Suggestions

- Using a Dictionary
- Reading from Parallel Translations
- Memorizing Scripture

Treasure Map

> All Scripture is breathed out by God and profitable for teaching, for reproof, for correction, and for training in righteousness.
>
> 2 TIMOTHY 3:16

Going Deep

Discovery

_____

_____

_____

_____

_____

_____

_____

_____

_____

_____

_____

_____

_____

_____

_____

_____

Tools for Digging

Tool Suggestions

- Praying the Scriptures
- Summarizing for the Big Picture
- Paraphrasing to Assimilate Truth

Treasure Map

I lift up my eyes to the hills.

From where does my help come?

My help comes from the Lord,

who made heaven and earth.

He will not let your foot be moved;

he who keeps you will not slumber.

Behold, he who keeps Israel

will neither slumber nor sleep.

The Lord is your keeper;

the Lord is your shade on your right hand.

The sun shall not strike you by day,

nor the moon by night.

The Lord will keep you from all evil;

he will keep your life.

The Lord will keep

your going out and your coming in

from this time forth and forevermore.

PSALM 121

Going Deep

_____
_____
_____
_____
_____
_____
_____

Discovery

_____
_____
_____
_____
_____
_____

Day 7 — *Tools for Digging*

Tool Suggestions

- Asking the Five W's and an H
- Marking and Color Coding
- Exploring Different Perspectives

Treasure Map

We do not want you to be uninformed, brothers, about those who are asleep, that you may not grieve as others do who have no hope. For since we believe that Jesus died and rose again, even so, through Jesus, God will bring with him those who have fallen asleep. For this we declare to you by a word from the Lord, that we who are alive, who are left until the coming of the Lord, will not precede those who have fallen asleep. For the Lord himself will descend from heaven with a cry of command, with the voice of an archangel, and with the sound of the trumpet of God. And the dead in Christ will rise first. Then we who are alive, who are left, will be caught up together with them in the clouds to meet the Lord in the air, and so we will always be with the Lord. Therefore encourage one another with these words.

1 Thessalonians 4:13–18

Going Deep

_____

_____

_____

_____

_____

_____

_____

_____

_____

_____

_____

_____

_____

_____

_____

_____

_____

_____

Month 3
Day 7 *Discovery*

_____
_____
_____
_____
_____
_____
_____
_____
_____
_____
_____
_____
_____
_____
_____
_____
_____
_____
_____

Tools for Digging

Tool Suggestions

- Paraphrasing to Assimilate Truth
- Teaching Your Children
- Meditating on God's Word

Treasure Map

Make a joyful noise to the Lord, all the earth!
Serve the Lord with gladness!
   Come into his presence with singing!

Know that the Lord, he is God!
   It is he who made us, and we are his;
   we are his people, and the sheep of his pasture.

Enter his gates with thanksgiving,
   and his courts with praise!
   Give thanks to him; bless his name!

For the Lord is good;
   his steadfast love endures forever,
   and his faithfulness to all generations.

PSALM 100

Going Deep

_____
_____
_____
_____
_____
_____
_____

Discovery

_____
_____
_____
_____
_____
_____

Day 9 | *Tools for Digging*

Tool Suggestions

- Making Practical Application
- Praying the Scriptures
- Marking and Color Coding

Treasure Map

Though the fig tree should not blossom,
nor fruit be on the vines,
the produce of the olive fail
and the fields yield no food,
the flock be cut off from the fold
and there be no herd in the stalls,
yet I will rejoice in the Lord;
I will take joy in the God of my salvation.
God, the Lord, is my strength;
he makes my feet like the deer's;
he makes me tread on my high places.

HABAKKUK 3:17–19

Going Deep

Month 3
Day 9 *Discovery*

_____

_____

_____

_____

_____

_____

_____

_____

_____

_____

_____

_____

_____

_____

_____

_____

_____

_____

Tools for Digging

Tool Suggestions

- Writing It Down and Walking It Out
- Reading Aloud and Emphasizing One Word at a Time
- Teaching Your Children

Treasure Map

God shows his love for us in that while we were still sinners, Christ died for us.

ROMANS 5:8

_____

_____

_____

_____

_____

_____

_____

_____

_____

_____

_____

_____

_____

_____

_____

_____

Discovery

Tools for Digging

Tool Suggestions

- Exploring Different Perspectives
- Investigating Original Languages
- Paraphrasing to Assimilate Truth

Treasure Map

Count it all joy, my brothers, when you meet trials of various kinds, for you know that the testing of your faith produces steadfastness.

JAMES 1:2–3

Going Deep

Tools for Digging

Tool Suggestions

- Using Your Imagination
- Studying Historical Contexts
- Writing It Down and Walking It Out

Treasure Map

> He told them another parable. "The kingdom of heaven is like leaven that a woman took and hid in three measures of flour, till it was all leavened."
>
> MATTHEW 13:33

Going Deep

Discovery

Tools for Digging

Tool Suggestions

- Using Your Imagination
- Paraphrasing to Assimilate Truth
- Looking for Rhema Rays

Treasure Map

The Lord is my shepherd; I shall not want.

He makes me lie down in green pastures.

He leads me beside still waters.

He restores my soul.

He leads me in paths of righteousness

for his name's sake.

Even though I walk through the valley of the
shadow of death,

I will fear no evil,

for you are with me;

your rod and your staff,

they comfort me.

You prepare a table before me

in the presence of my enemies;

you anoint my head with oil;

my cup overflows.

Surely goodness and mercy shall follow me

all the days of my life,

and I shall dwell in the house of the Lord forever.

PSALM 23

Going Deep

_____

_____

_____

_____

_____

_____

Discovery

_____

_____

_____

_____

_____

Tools for Digging

Tool Suggestions

- Asking the Five W's and an H
- Reading from Parallel Translations
- Using a Dictionary

Treasure Map

> Jesus came and said to them, "All authority in heaven and on earth has been given to me. Go therefore and make disciples of all nations, baptizing them in the name of the Father and of the Son and of the Holy Spirit, teaching them to observe all that I have commanded you. And behold, I am with you always, to the end of the age."
>
> MATTHEW 28:18–20

Going Deep

_____

_____

_____

_____

_____

_____

_____

_____

_____

_____

_____

_____

_____

_____

_____

_____

Discovery

Tools for Digging

Tool Suggestions

- Memorizing Scripture
- Teaching Your Children
- Making Practical Application

Treasure Map

If possible, so far as it depends on you, live peaceably with all.

ROMANS 12:18

Going Deep

_____

_____

_____

_____

_____

_____

_____

_____

_____

_____

_____

_____

_____

_____

_____

_____

_____

_____

_____

_____

_____

_____

_____

_____

_____

_____

_____

_____

_____

_____

_____

_____

_____

Tools for Digging

Tool Suggestions

- Exploring Different Perspectives
- Using Your Imagination
- Summarizing for the Big Picture

When Joseph's brothers saw that their father was dead, they said, "It may be that Joseph will hate us and pay us back for all the evil that we did to him." So they sent a message to Joseph, saying, "Your father gave this command before he died, 'Say to Joseph, Please forgive the transgression of your brothers and their sin, because they did evil to you.' And now, please forgive the transgression of the servants of the God of your father." Joseph wept when they spoke to him. His brothers also came and fell down before him and said, "Behold, we are your servants." But Joseph said to them, "Do not fear, for am I in the place of God? As for you, you meant evil against me, but God meant it for good, to bring it about that many people should be kept alive, as they are today. So do not fear; I will provide for you and your little ones." Thus he comforted them and spoke kindly to them.

GENESIS 50:15–21

Going Deep

_____

_____

_____

_____

_____

_____

_____

Discovery

_____

_____

_____

_____

_____

_____

Day 17 | Tools for Digging

Tool Suggestions

- Studying Historical Contexts
- Choosing a Topical Study
- Memorizing Scripture

Treasure Map

> You are the salt of the earth, but if salt has lost its taste, how shall its saltiness be restored? It is no longer good for anything except to be thrown out and trampled under people's feet.
>
> You are the light of the world. A city set on a hill cannot be hidden. Nor do people light a lamp and put it under a basket, but on a stand, and it gives light to all in the house. In the same way, let your light shine before others, so that they may see your good works and give glory to your Father who is in heaven.
>
> MATTHEW 5:13–16

Going Deep

_____

_____

_____

_____

_____

_____

_____

_____

_____

_____

_____

_____

_____

_____

_____

_____

_____

_____

Tools for Digging

Tool Suggestions

- Reading Aloud and Emphasizing One Word at a Time
- Reading from Parallel Translations
- Choosing a Topical Study

Treasure Map

> Give all your worries and cares to God, for he cares about you.
>
> 1 PETER 5:7 NLT

_____

_____

_____

_____

_____

_____

_____

_____

_____

_____

_____

_____

_____

_____

_____

_____

_____

Discovery

Tools for Digging

Tool Suggestions

- "Interviewing" through Biographical Study
- Investigating Original Languages
- Summarizing for the Big Picture

Treasure Map

Thomas, one of the Twelve, called the Twin, was not with them when Jesus came. So the other disciples told him, "We have seen the Lord." But he said to them, "Unless I see in his hands the mark of the nails, and place my finger into the mark of the nails, and place my hand into his side, I will never believe."

Eight days later, his disciples were inside again, and Thomas was with them. Although the doors were locked, Jesus came and stood among them and said, "Peace be with you." Then he said to Thomas, "Put your finger here, and see my hands; and put out your hand, and place it in my side. Do not disbelieve, but believe." Thomas answered him, "My Lord and my God!"

JOHN 20:24–28

Going Deep

Month 3
Day 19 *Discovery*

_____

_____

_____

_____

_____

_____

_____

_____

_____

_____

_____

_____

_____

_____

_____

_____

Tools for Digging

Tool Suggestions

- Looking for Rhema Rays
- Reading from Parallel Translations
- Paraphrasing to Assimilate Truth

Treasure Map

To him who is able to keep you from stumbling and to present you blameless before the presence of his glory with great joy, to the only God, our Savior, through Jesus Christ our Lord, be glory, majesty, dominion, and authority, before all time and now and forever. Amen.

JUDE 24–25

233

Discovery

Appendix

Web Sites

http://bible.com
http://bible.lifeway.com
http://crosswalk.com
http://studylight.org
http://www.biblegateway.com
http://www.gospelcom.net

Bible Software

Logos Bible Software
e-Sword
BibleWorks
QuickVerse
WORDsearch

Bible Study Tools

Commentaries

New Bible Commentary: 21st Century Edition
The Bible Knowledge Commentary
New American Commentary

Study Bibles

Spirit-Filled Life Study Bible (NKJV)
The Nelson Study Bible (NKJV)
The Woman's Study Bible (NKJV)

Appendix

Word Dictionaries

The Complete Word Study Dictionary: Old Testament
The Complete Word Study Dictionary: New Testament
Theological Wordbook of the Old Testament
Vine's Complete Expository Dictionary of Old and New Testament Words

Bible Dictionaries

New Bible Dictionary, third edition
Nelson's New Illustrated Bible Dictionary

Bible Encyclopedias

The International Standard Bible Encyclopedia
Baker Encyclopedia of the Bible

Bible Handbooks

The Hayford Bible Handbook
Willmington's Bible Handbook

Lexicons

A Greek-English Lexicon of the New Testament and Other Early Christian Literature, third edition
Enhanced Brown-Driver-Briggs Hebrew and English Lexicon

Concordances

New American Standard Updated Edition Exhaustive Concordance of the Bible
Strong's Exhaustive Concordance of the Bible

Appendix

Cross-reference Books

The New Treasury of Scripture Knowledge

Nave's Topical Bible

Interlinear Bibles

The English-Hebrew Reverse Interlinear Old Testament

The English-Greek Reverse Interlinear New Testament

Manners and Customs Books

Nelson's New Illustrated Bible Manners and Customs

Notes

1. "How does a person meditate on God's Word?" *NIV Quest Study Bible, Revised* (Grand Rapids: Zondervan, 2003), note on Psalm 119:15.

2. I highly recommend Memlock (www.Memlock.com), a Scripture memorization software program that provides these pictures for you.

3. Kenneth S. Wuest, *Word Studies in the Greek New Testament* (Grand Rapids: Eerdmans, 1997).

4. Spiros Zodhiates, *The Complete Word Study Dictionary: New Testament* (electronic ed.) (Chattanooga, TN: AMG, 2000), G3056.

5. By permission. From Merriam-Webster's Collegiate® Dictionary, Eleventh Edition © 2006 by Merriam-Webster, Incorporated (www.Merriam-Webster.com).

6. J. R. Dummelow, ed., *The One Volume Bible Commentary* (New York: Macmillan, 1974).

7. Bruce B. Barton, *Life Application Bible Commentary, Matthew* (Wheaton, IL: Tyndale, 1996), 221.

8. Craig Blomberg, *Matthew*, vol. 22 of *The New American Commentary*, electronic ed., Logos Library System (Nashville: Broadman & Holman, 2001), 185.

9. Vance H. Havner, *Though I Walk Through the Valley* (Old Tappan, NJ: Revell, 1974), 62.

About the Author

Lisa Whelchel is best known for her role as Blair on the long-running television comedy *The Facts of Life*. Now a homeschooling mother, speaker, and pastor's wife, she is the best-selling author of *Creative Correction*; *Taking Care of the Me in Mommy*; *The Facts of Life and Other Lessons My Father Taught Me*; *So You're Thinking About Homeschooling*; *The Busy Mom's Guide to Prayer*; *The Busy Mom's Guide to Wisdom*; and coauthor of *The Busy Grandma's Guide to Prayer*. Lisa and her husband, Steve, are the cofounders of MomTime Ministries. They live in Texas with their children Tucker, Haven, and Clancy. For more information about Lisa, visit www.LisaWhelchel.com.

The Busy Mom's
Guide to
Prayer

A GUIDED PRAYER JOURNAL

Lisa Whelchel

$\mathcal{L}isa\ \mathcal{W}helchel$ is best known for her role as "Blair" on the long-running television comedy *The Facts of Life*. Now a homeschooling mother, speaker, and pastor's wife, she is the best-selling author of *Creative Correction, The Facts of Life and Other Lessons My Father Taught Me,* and *So, You're Thinking About Homeschooling.* Lisa and her husband, Steve, are the cofounders of MomTime Ministries. They live in Texas with their children Tucker, Haven, and Clancy. www.LisaWhelchel.com

What an honor to dedicate this book
to a couple of prayer warriors,
Reverend Curtis and Reverend Alice Cauble.
Thank you for the venerable heritage you pass down
to Tucker, Haven, and Clancy through your life, prayers,
and son, my wonderful husband, Steven.

Those who are planted in the house of the LORD shall flourish in the
courts of our God. They shall still bear fruit in old age;
they shall be fresh and flourishing.
—Psalm 92:13–14 NKJV

Our purpose at Howard Publishing is to:

- *Increase faith* in the hearts of growing Christians
- *Inspire holiness* in the lives of believers
- *Instill hope* in the hearts of struggling people everywhere

Because He's coming again!

The Busy Mom's Guide to Prayer © 2005 by Lisa Whelchel
All rights reserved. Printed in the United States of America
Published by Howard Publishing Co., Inc.
3117 North 7th Street, West Monroe, Louisiana 71291-2227
www.howardpublishing.com

09 10 11 12 13 14   10 9 8 7 6 5 4 3 2

Edited by Philis Boultinghouse
Interior design by Stephanie D. Walker
Cover design by Cindy Sartain and Stephanie D. Walker
Illustrations by Cindy Sartain

ISBN: 1-4165-3379-6

Contents

Contents

Day 5

Day 6

Day 7

Day 8

Day 9

Day 10

Day 11

Day 12

Contents

Day 17

Day 18

Day 19

Day 20

Acknowledgments

Without the help of the following people, I absolutely could not have written *The Busy Mom's Guide to Prayer*!

This has been a remarkably easy and pleasant writing experience. That has everything to do with the genuine and gracious people working at the godly company Howard Publishing. Thank you, Philis, Denny, Chrys, and John. I've loved every minute working with you. (And I believe we had about thirty minutes in all to get this book ready, didn't we?)

Over the last twenty years, Stormie Omartian has played a pivotal role in my life at many transitional moments. Thank you, Stormie, for mentoring a shy girl, frightened wife, overwhelmed mother, and needy friend with the power of prayer.

It doesn't make sense to me why I feel so emotionally connected with friends I've never even met. But I like it! Thank you, Cyber Friends, for joining me on Monday mornings on my Web site for Coffee Talks. You have encouraged me more times than I can enumerate.

I still feel like such "weak sauce" (to use my son's vernacular) when it comes to prayer. I've come to desperately depend on the prompting of the Holy Spirit on other people's hearts. Thank you, Prayer Warriors, who have responded to the call when God has quickened to your hearts that I need supernatural help.

Have I mentioned how much I love Logos Bible Software? I can't even imagine how much time it would have taken me to find almost two hundred scriptures without this phenomenal program. And I had so much fun searching for the buried treasures within God's Word.

Acknowledgments

Thank you, Scott Lindsey and Libronix, for providing more than six hundred Bible resources at my mouse click.

Thanks, Ron, for keeping it fun. You're the man!(-ager)

I can never pass up an opportunity to mention my gorgeous husband and adorable children. Thank you, Steve, Tucker, Haven, and Clancy, for giving me so much to pray about—it keeps me close to my Sweet Jesus. I love you, love you, love you!

Introduction

My heart's desire is to be a woman of prayer, but more often than not, I feel like a failure as a pray-er. As a busy mom, it is sometimes all I can do to cry out to the Lord at sunrise with a quick, "Help me!" before the *son rise*s inside the house and my girls start crying out to me with the same plea.

If I miss my quiet-time window of opportunity in the morning, the shattering of that pane is immediately felt as I realize that there is very little chance for peace and quiet until after everyone is in bed. (That is, of course, after the second drink of water and the third good-night kiss.) By that time I'm typically so exhausted I can barely whisper, "I'm sorry, Lord. I promise to do better tomorrow."

With sincere resolve I begin the next day on my knees covering my family in prayer only to find my wandering mind suddenly thinking thoughts like, "Oh no, we only have crusts left to make sandwiches for lunch." "Did they cancel baseball practice today?" "I can't forget to write a note for this afternoon's orthodontist appointment." "Oh, I'm sorry, Lord, now where were we?"

My prayers are broken into yet again, but this time by an audible voice, "Mom, I can't find my science homework. Where did you put it?" *Where did I put it? It is your responsibility to keep up with your own . . .* And we're off! Another race against the clock with only seconds to spare for a few "popcorn prayers" shot up to the Lord throughout one more busy day in the life of a mom.

A Busy Mother
—An Understanding Father

I truly believe that God understands this unique season in a mother's life. Thankfully, our heavenly Father looks on the hearts of mothers with compassion and understanding. He is not peering down, shaking His head with a "Tsk, tsk, I guess I'm going to have to give her a miserable day because she didn't get the requisite amount of prayer time logged."

Remembering the merciful character of God has comforted me on many occasions when the enemy has attempted to hammer me with feelings of guilt because I wasn't the prayer warrior I wanted to be. In my estimation I was a "General" in the Lord's army. Not because I had earned the highest ranking for a soldier but because it seemed it was all I could do to find enough time for even general prayers. "Lord, bless my husband today. Help my children in school. Please provide the money we need to pay all of our bills. And help me to be the wife and mother You want me to be. In Jesus's name, amen."

God hears those prayers, and He answers them! But I desperately wanted more. I longed for the time to pray for details like my husband's personal walk with the Lord and his relationships with his coworkers. I wanted to saturate my children in prayer for their future and matters of the heart. I felt guilty for not praying for my pastor and the president. And when I told friends, "I'll pray for you," I really did mean to do just that.

Introduction

I always had the best of intentions to pray for all these things. But you've probably heard the ugly adage, "The pathway to hell is paved with good intentions." I decided I didn't like that saying (even if it did contain a nugget of truth), so I created my own personal prayer binder and titled it *The Pathway to Heaven Is Prayed with Good Intentions.*

Wrapping My World

On individual slips of paper, I wrote down everything and everyone I would ever want to pray for. I came up with around three hundred different prayer concerns, and I organized them into ten categories. By praying for one thing from each category every day, I was able to cover all three hundred prayer needs in one month! I felt like a bona fide prayer warrior.

It felt so good to know that once a month I would cover health for my husband, purity for my children, diet struggles for me, prayers for my friends, relatives, and even Jerusalem. All I needed was ten minutes a day, and I could pray for the world, and more specifically, my world. There were even some days when I got carried away and realized I had been praying for thirty minutes without looking at my watch or refereeing a sibling argument.

This prayer system transformed my own life so much that I couldn't wait to share it with my online friends through my Web site. Over the next few days and months, I received tons of excited e-mails from moms everywhere who were using this method. They shared the joy and peace they experienced, knowing their lives, though busy, were wrapped in prayer.

Miracle Minutes

The Busy Mom's Guide to Prayer is the result of my desire to create a product moms could pick up and immediately jump right into enjoying a fulfilling (full and filling!) life of prayer. All you need is a few minutes a day, five days a week and voila—out with the guilt and in with the power! This book has been adapted from my home-made version to make it versatile enough to fit *your* prayer needs.

You will notice that the book has twenty days of prayer. You can use these twenty days anytime that works best for you, but the idea is that there are prayer guidelines for five days a week for a month. Then when the first month is over, you can do what I do with my prayer guide and start over again. The prayers outlined in this book need to be lifted up over and over again.

Each day has six prayer categories. Each category begins with a *Scripture Inspiration* and a section for *Praying the Word.* I have discovered that it is much easier for me to pray with faith when I can ground my requests in the promises of God. There is an immeasurable dimension of anointing that comes along with lining our words up with the Word of God.

The *Prayer Prompt* can be interpreted two ways. If you can only steal a few minutes to pray while waiting in the carpool lane at school, then *promptly* repeat the suggested prayers and rest easy

Introduction

knowing your concerns are covered. If, on the other hand, you would like to linger on a particular petition then simply use the proposed prayer as a springboard, or *prompt*, to dive into deeper conversation with the Lord.

I have chosen six of the most mom-requested categories. They are *Praise, Self, Husband, Children, Personal Influences,* and *Reaching Beyond*. Beginning on day 1, I have broken each of these down even further into twenty *prayer focuses*—one focus per day.

For instance, on the very first day, in the *Praise* category, you will begin praising the Lord for His holiness. Then, in the *Self* category, you will pray for wisdom; godly priorities in the *Husband* category; future spouse in the *Children* category; the personal needs of your pastor in the *Personal Influences* category; and finally, you'll conclude by lifting up the president of the United States in the *Reaching Beyond* category.

Categorically Speaking

Indulge me for a couple of pages while I share my passion in choosing each of these six categories. I love to begin with *Praise* because it helps to put my prayer requests in perspective. As I exalt the multifaceted, brilliant radiance of the character of God, my concerns become both significant and trivial at the same time. The God of the universe cares enough to ask me to bring my biggest concerns before Him so they can shrink in His presence.

Most moms put everybody else's needs before their own, and yet when it comes to prayer, it is critical that we put our *Self* first. Giving is part of the very makeup of a mother (the foundation, perhaps), but we must remember that we cannot give that which we haven't received. This isn't selfish; it is reality. Our relationship with God affects every other relationship in our lives. This is our chance to go deeper with the Lord than ever before, to know Him intimately. Get brutally honest, take any masks off, and let's ask the Chief Physician to perform an extreme makeover so we can look more like Jesus.

First Peter 3:1 says, "Wives, likewise, be submissive to your own husbands, that even if some do not obey the word, they, without a word may be won by the conduct of their wives" (NKJV). I really have a hard time with that scripture, not the part about submission, the *without a word* phrase. I have so much to say to (and about) my husband if he would only listen to me. Thankfully, God does listen—not to what I say, but to what I pray for my *Husband.* What a gift we can give the men we love when we trust God to impress upon their hearts from the inside-out, rather than trying to change them by applying pressure from the outside-in.

Is there any prayer more readily on our lips than those for our *Children*? I think controlling mothers sometimes get a bad rap. After all, it is only because we care so much. When our kids are little we worry about protecting them from others. Once they hit the teenage years, we worry about protecting them from themselves. Either way, we quickly discover that we can't control everything that

Introduction

happens to our children. But that doesn't mean we can't give it our best shot through prayer. Praying for our children is a constant balancing act between handing them over to the Lord and seizing the best for them in the Spirit. I think we are up to the task, don't you, Mom?

You may be surprised at how many *Personal Influences* touch you on any given day. Think about the people who impact your life: teachers, pastors, coworkers. Now think of the lives you have the power to influence: neighbors, friends, unsaved acquaintances. We have the opportunity to not only reach out to those around us with the love of Jesus but to also leave an eternal impression on them by inviting God's touch on their lives through prayer.

Talking with God really gets fun when we begin *Reaching Beyond* our immediate sphere of influence to include the whole globe. Can you imagine being given the power within your own praying hands to change the world? Tends to make that extra five minutes of sleep a little less essential, doesn't it? What was God thinking when He gave us that much power? Maybe it was, "If My people who are called by My name will humble themselves, and pray and seek My face, and turn from their wicked ways, then I will hear from heaven, and will forgive their sin and heal their land" (2 Chronicles 7:14 NKJV).

Filling in the Blanks

I have chosen the first six categories for you, but remember, this journal is *your* personal journey. (Would that make it a *journey-al*?)

Introduction

We've left lots of blank lines for your own prayers. Use this space however you feel led. You may want to expand and expound on the pre-existing categories or add new categories of your own. Perhaps you want to leave them open to add random prayer requests that come up along the way. Many of you will have particular prayer needs that you can fill in that are especially close to your heart.

In my own personal prayer journal, I have added prayer focuses for co-laborers, specific aspects of my ministry, and an entire category just to pray for each of my extended family members. I love my friend Philis's idea of interviewing her relatives. When she put together her prayer journal, she called her mother, father, brothers, sisters, nieces, nephews, and in-laws and asked them how she could specifically pray for each one of them.

No matter how somebody feels about God, it is a rare person who will pass up the offer to be prayed for. Take advantage of this open door to their hearts and bring their needs and desires to your heavenly Father on their behalf. Perhaps when He opens those doors and answers their prayers, they will invite Him in.

A List of Prayer Lists

I'm confident you will be able to come up with plenty of ways to personalize this prayer journal. To get your creative juices pumping, here are just a few additional categories and prayer focuses.

- **Your Church**—pastors, building fund, elders, choir, youth, programs, unity, etc.

Introduction

- **Small Group Members**—MOPS, Bible study, home groups, MomTime Friends, etc.

- **Large Ministries**—Focus on the Family, crisis pregnancy centers, Joni & Friends, etc.

- **Churches in the City**—all denominations in your community

- **Neighbors**—each family (by name) on your block or apartment

- **People Who Serve You**—grocery checker, dry cleaner, cashier, hair dresser, mail deliverer, etc.

- **People Who Influence Your Children**—teachers, coaches, bullies, youth workers, etc.

- **Your Calendar**—this day next month, to level the mountains ahead of time, etc.

- **Current Events**—news headlines, weather traumas, victims, unsolved crimes, etc.

Prayer Request List

- **The Sick**—infirm, elderly, hospitalized, diseased, and shut-ins, etc.

- **Prominent Ministers**—Dr. James Dobson, Billy Graham, James Robison, Jack Hayford, etc.

- **Personal Impact**—Beth Moore, Stormie Omartian, Francine Rivers, Elisabeth Elliot, etc.

- **Your Children's Friends and Their Parents**

- **Yours or Your Husband's Coworkers**

- **Unsaved Friends**

Introduction

- Celebrities/Athletes/Personalities—any whom God puts on your heart
- Political Issues
- Grandchildren
- Blended Families—ex-wives, ex-husbands, stepchildren, stepparents, etc.

Personal Ministry Involvements

- The Needy—poor, persecuted, laborers, defenseless, prisoners, victims of crime, etc.
- Missionaries
- "10/40 Window" Nations
- Patients—Alzheimer's, cancer, coma, diabetes, multiple sclerosis, heart disease, etc.
- Other Religions—Muslims, Scientologists, Atheists, New Age, etc.
- School—principal, teachers, PTA, school board, etc.
- Homeschool Issues—curriculum choices, extra-curricular activities, the teacher! etc.

On Your Knees . . . Get Set . . . Pray

"They shall run and not be weary." Now there is a promise every mother needs to hold on to for dear life. What is the secret to avoiding mom burnout? It is tucked away within the first part of that particular scripture, Isaiah 40:31, "Those who wait on the LORD shall renew their strength" (NKJV).

Introduction

Now that you hold this book in your hands, I think it will be easier to find times of refreshing in your day to wait on the Lord and cast your burdens upon Him. Not because there is anything particularly special about this prayer journal but because sometimes all it takes to dig a little deeper is the right tool. Besides, I know your heart is to be a woman of prayer. And when your heart is in the right place, it is inevitable that the *rest* will follow.

I italicized "rest" because Hebrews 4:10 tells us, "For he who has entered His rest has himself also ceased from his works as God did from His" (NKJV). We don't have to worry when we are confident that God is working on our behalf in response to our prayers. As moms we can run around all day, fall into bed exhausted, and still experience the peace that passes understanding. Where have I heard that phrase before?

Oh yeah, Philippians 4:6–7 NKJV—"Be anxious for nothing, but in everything by prayer and supplication, with thanksgiving, let your requests be made known to God; and the peace of God, which surpasses all understanding, will guard your hearts and minds through Christ Jesus."

Hey, Mom, that's another good promise to hold on to. Let us pray.

Praise

☕ **Prayer Focus**—Holiness

📖 **Scripture Inspiration**

There is no one holy like the LORD, indeed there is no one besides You. (1 Samuel 2:2 NASB)

⊚ **Praying the Word**

Most Holy Lord, there is no one as wonderful and perfect as You; You are the one God, and no one else even comes close to You.

❀ **Prayer Prompt**

Thank You for the privilege of joining with the voices of heaven as we cry, "Holy, holy, holy, Lord God Almighty, who was and is and is to come." You are worthy of my complete devotion because You are perfect in goodness and righteousness.

Prayer Focus

Scripture Inspiration

_____
_____
_____
_____

Praying the Word

_____
_____
_____
_____
_____

Prayer Prompt

_____
_____
_____
_____
_____
_____
_____
_____
_____

Day 1

Self

📖 Scripture Inspiration

If any of you lacks wisdom, let him ask God, who gives generously to all without reproach, and it will be given him. (James 1:5 ESV)

☉ Praying the Word

God, I need wisdom and a lot of it. I know You don't think badly of me when I admit that I don't know what to do. As a matter of fact, You are just waiting for me to ask You for wisdom so You can give me all that I need.

❀ Prayer Prompt

There are times when I simply don't know what to do, where to go, or what to say. I don't want to rely on my own limited ability to figure out what is best. I humbly submit to Your will and ask You to give me Your wisdom. Help me make decisions that align with Your will.

Prayer Focus_____

Scripture Inspiration

_____
_____
_____
_____

Praying the Word

_____
_____
_____
_____
_____
_____

Prayer Prompt

_____
_____
_____
_____
_____
_____
_____
_____
_____
_____

Day 1

Husband

☕ **Prayer Focus**—Priorities

📖 **Scripture Inspiration**

But seek first the kingdom of God and his righteousness, and all these things will be added to you. (Matthew 6:33 ESV)

⊙ **Praying the Word**

Dear Lord, remind my husband not to worry about the things of this world but to keep his focus on knowing You and obeying You, trusting that You will provide everything we need.

🌸 **Prayer Prompt**

Give my husband an eternal perspective. Open his eyes to see that the only thing we can take with us to heaven is people. Encourage him to invest in our marriage and family, and reveal to him the intangible dividends that are reaped. Remind him that You are ultimately our Provider and You will take care of all our needs. Mostly, give him a hunger and thirst to spend time with You more every day.

Prayer Focus _____

Scripture Inspiration

_____

_____

_____

_____

Praying the Word

_____

_____

_____

_____

_____

_____

Prayer Prompt

_____

_____

_____

_____

_____

_____

_____

_____

_____

_____

Day 1
Children

☕ **Prayer Focus**—Future Spouse

📖 **Scripture Inspiration**

He who finds a wife finds a good thing and obtains favor from the LORD. (Proverbs 18:22 ESV)

◎ **Praying the Word**

Dear Lord, I ask You to show favor upon my children and help them to find the spouses You have chosen for them.

❀ **Prayer Prompt**

Heavenly Father, I lift up my children's future spouses to You and ask that You will guard, protect, and keep them from the evil one and from all impurity. I pray for their parents and ask You to strengthen their marriage so they will be raised in a strong, godly home. Shape and mold them by Your Holy Spirit, and help them to stay on Your path so they may find the destiny You have prepared for their future.

Prayer Focus _____

Scripture Inspiration

_____
_____
_____
_____

Praying the Word

_____
_____
_____
_____
_____
_____

Prayer Prompt

_____
_____
_____
_____
_____
_____
_____
_____
_____
_____

9

Day 1

Personal Influences

☕ **Prayer Focus**–Senior Pastor

📖 **Scripture Inspiration**
Shepherd the flock of God which is among you, serving as overseers, not by compulsion but willingly, not for dishonest gain but eagerly. (1 Peter 5:2 NKJV)

🕮 **Praying the Word**
Jesus, You are the Chief Shepherd, and I ask You to lead my pastor as he leads our church. Give him fresh excitement and enthusiasm for the work he is called to do.

🌸 **Prayer Prompt**
Thank You, Lord, for my pastor. Please bless his home, marriage, and family. Give him times of refreshing with You so that his words will flow out of power-full times spent in Your Word.

Reaching Beyond

☕ **Prayer Focus**–The President

📖 **Scripture Inspiration**
The king's heart is in the hand of the LORD, like the rivers of water; He turns it wherever He wishes. (Proverbs 21:1 NKJV)

🕮 **Praying the Word**
Dear Lord, hold the heart of our country's leader in Your hand. Channel his thoughts, feelings, and decisions.

🌸 **Prayer Prompt**
Thank You for our president. Protect him and fill him with supernatural wisdom and guidance. Teach him to walk in humility and to seek You for direction and wisdom.

☕ **Prayer Focus**_____

📖 Scripture Inspiration

_____

_____

🕐 Praying the Word

_____

_____

🌸 Prayer Prompt

_____

_____

_____

☕ **Prayer Focus**_____

📖 Scripture Inspiration

_____

_____

🕐 Praying the Word

_____

_____

🌸 Prayer Prompt

_____

_____

_____

Day 2

Praise

☕ **Prayer Focus**—Mercy

📖 **Scripture Inspiration**

Blessed be the God and Father of our Lord Jesus Christ, the Father of mercies and God of all comfort. (2 Corinthians 1:3 NKJV)

☺ **Praying the Word**

God and Father of our Lord Jesus Christ, You are worthy of worship. We are comforted by You because You have reconciled us through Your Son.

🌸 **Prayer Prompt**

I am so grateful for Your mercy. In my sin I am deserving of judgment, but You have not only redeemed me by the blood of Jesus but You've embraced me and pulled me near. Because of Your mercy, I can come boldly before the throne of grace.

☕ Prayer Focus_____

📖 Scripture Inspiration

_____
_____
_____
_____

🌀 Praying the Word

_____
_____
_____
_____
_____
_____

🌸 Prayer Prompt

_____
_____
_____
_____
_____
_____
_____
_____
_____

Day 2

Self

📖 Scripture Inspiration

Therefore, just as the church is subject to Christ, so let the wives be to their own husbands in everything. And let the wife see that she respects her husband. (Ephesians 5:24, 33 ESV)

☉ Praying the Word

Dear Jesus, I submit myself to You as my authority. Help me to recognize my husband as the head of our family and to accept his leadership. Help me show my husband the respect that his position in our home deserves.

🌸 Prayer Prompt

I understand that my respect ministers to my husband even more than my love for him does. Show me how I can build him up and put a guard on my mouth when I'm tempted to tear him down. Love my husband through me, and teach me to enjoy finding ways to serve him throughout the day (and night).

☕ Prayer Focus_____

📖 Scripture Inspiration

_____
_____
_____
_____

☺ Praying the Word

_____
_____
_____
_____
_____
_____

🌸 Prayer Prompt

_____
_____
_____
_____
_____
_____
_____
_____
_____
_____
_____

Day 2
Husband

☕ **Prayer Focus**—Daily Devotions

📖 **Scripture Inspiration**

How can a young man keep his way pure? By guarding it according to your word. With my whole heart I seek you; let me not wander from your commandments! (Psalm 119:9–10 ESV)

☺ Praying the Word

Put a deep desire in my husband's heart to seek You. Teach him to cling to Your commandments and obey them, for that is how he will remain safe and sinless.

❀ Prayer Prompt

Draw my husband closer to You. Give him a hunger and thirst to spend time with You daily. May he look forward to his set time with You to share his heart, unload his burdens, and communicate with You in prayer. Open the Scriptures to him with such a fresh revelation that he can't wait to hear what You want to speak to him every day.

☕ Prayer Focus _____

📖 Scripture Inspiration

_____
_____
_____
_____

✆ Praying the Word

_____
_____
_____
_____
_____
_____

🌸 Prayer Prompt

_____
_____
_____
_____
_____
_____
_____
_____
_____
_____

Day 2
Children

☕ **Prayer Focus**—Siblings

📖 **Scripture Inspiration**

Finally, all of you be of one mind, having compassion for one another; love as brothers, be tenderhearted, be courteous; not returning evil for evil or reviling for reviling, but on the contrary blessing, knowing that you were called to this, that you may inherit a blessing. (1 Peter 3:8–9 NKJV)

☺ **Praying the Word**

Father, I pray for a blessing on our home. I ask for unity, sincere love for each other, gratefulness for the privilege of siblings, kindness, and sensitivity. I ask You to grant my children self-control not to respond tit-for-tat or add insult to injury, but instead, to overcome evil with good.

❀ **Prayer Prompt**

O Lord, grant peace to this family. May the sweetness of the Holy Spirit permeate every inch of this household. Enable my children to encourage one another, cherish one another, and be quick to forgive and be merciful. Help them to be slow to speak, slow to anger, and willing to listen. Make my children each other's best friends.

Prayer Focus _____

Scripture Inspiration

_____
_____
_____
_____

Praying the Word

_____
_____
_____
_____
_____
_____

Prayer Prompt

_____
_____
_____
_____
_____
_____
_____
_____
_____

Day 2

Personal Influences

☕ **Prayer Focus**–Youth Pastor

📖 **Scripture Inspiration**

When I was a child, I spoke like a child, I thought like a child, I reasoned like a child. When I became a man, I gave up childish ways. (1 Corinthians 13:11 ESV)

☉ **Praying the Word**

Guide our youth pastor as he leads our children into young adulthood. Show him how to teach them to leave childish things behind and embrace the responsibilities and privileges of being an adult.

🌼 **Prayer Prompt**

Strengthen our youth pastor's personal relationship with You so he may model true discipleship to his young flock.

Reaching Beyond

☕ **Prayer Focus**–America

📖 **Scripture Inspiration**

If my people . . . pray and seek my face and turn from their wicked ways, then I will hear from heaven and will forgive their sin and heal their land. (2 Chronicles 7:14 ESV)

☉ **Praying the Word**

We humbly kneel before You with repentant hearts and ask You to forgive our sins and heal our nation.

🌼 **Prayer Prompt**

Thank You for the favor that is upon us. Lead us by Your right hand. God bless America.

☕ Prayer Focus _____

📖 Scripture Inspiration

_____

_____

◎ Praying the Word

_____

_____

❀ Prayer Prompt

_____

_____

_____

☕ Prayer Focus _____

📖 Scripture Inspiration

_____

_____

◎ Praying the Word

_____

_____

❀ Prayer Prompt

_____

_____

_____

Praise

☕ **Prayer Focus**—Faithfulness

📖Scripture Inspiration

I will sing of the loving kindness of the Lord forever; To all generations I will make known Your faithfulness with my mouth. (Psalm 89:1 NASB)

☺ Praying the Word

I will sing of Your loving kindness forever, Lord, and I will personally tell everyone about Your faithfulness to me.

✿ Prayer Prompt

Even when I don't have any faith, You are still faithful. Your love and commitment never change. You have never let me down in the past, and I know I can trust You for the future. I will rest in You and Your character.

Prayer Focus _____

Scripture Inspiration

_____
_____
_____
_____

Praying the Word

_____
_____
_____
_____
_____
_____

Prayer Prompt

_____
_____
_____
_____
_____
_____
_____
_____
_____

Day 3
Self

☕ **Prayer Focus**—Role as Mother

📖 Scripture Inspiration

You shall teach them diligently to your children, and shall talk of them when you sit in your house, and when you walk by the way, and when you lie down, and when you rise.
(Deuteronomy 6:7 ESV)

☺ Praying the Word

Dear heavenly Father, write Your Word on my heart so that Your wisdom simply flows from my mouth throughout the day that I might teach my children Your ways.

🌸 Prayer Prompt

Thank You for the privilege of being a mother and for the precious gifts You've entrusted to me. Let me begin by giving them back to You; they are safer in Your strong and loving hands. Anoint me to teach, train, and love my children beyond my human capabilities. Make me the mother You've specifically created me to be for these particular children.

☕ Prayer Focus_____

📖 Scripture Inspiration

_____
_____
_____
_____

🌀 Praying the Word

_____
_____
_____
_____
_____
_____

🌸 Prayer Prompt

_____
_____
_____
_____
_____
_____
_____
_____
_____

Day 3
Husband

☕ **Prayer Focus**—Role as Husband

📖 **Scripture Inspiration**

Husbands, love your wives, as Christ loved the church and gave himself up for her. (Ephesians 5:25 ESV)

☺ **Praying the Word**

Jesus, fill my husband's heart with Your love for me, and show him how to love me with the same kind of sacrificial love You have for him.

🌸 **Prayer Prompt**

I know my husband loves me and he desires to serve me and make me happy. Thank You for that. Make him the husband that he longs to be and that I need. Help me to remember to encourage him as he reaches out to show his love, whether in words or actions. Teach him how to care for me with as much attention as he would show himself.

Prayer Focus_____

Scripture Inspiration

_____

_____

_____

_____

Praying the Word

_____

_____

_____

_____

_____

_____

Prayer Prompt

_____

_____

_____

_____

_____

_____

_____

_____

_____

Day 3
Children

☕ **Prayer Focus**—Respect for Authority

📖 **Scripture Inspiration**

The fear of the LORD is the beginning of knowledge, but fools despise wisdom and instruction. (Proverbs 1:7 NKJV)

☺ **Praying the Word**

Lord, grant my children a healthy respect for Your authority. Teach them to love knowledge, seek wisdom, and obey instruction.

❧ **Prayer Prompt**

Instill in my children a right understanding of the blessing of authority. May they enjoy the safety and protection that comes from submitting to those over them. Give them a teachable spirit that is open to learning from the wisdom of others. Teach them to honor You, their parents, those placed in positions above them, and the elderly.

Prayer Focus _____

Scripture Inspiration

_____

_____

_____

_____

Praying the Word

_____

_____

_____

_____

_____

_____

Prayer Prompt

_____

_____

_____

_____

_____

_____

_____

_____

_____

_____

Day 3

Personal Influences

☕ **Prayer Focus**–Sunday School Teachers

📖 **Scripture Inspiration**

The things that you have heard from me among many witnesses, commit these to faithful men who will be able to teach others also. (2 Timothy 2:2 NKJV)

🌀 **Praying the Word**

Continue to speak to our Sunday School teachers so they may faithfully pass on what they are learning from You.

🌸 **Prayer Prompt**

Raise up Sunday School teachers who are called to teach and disciple adults and love and train children. As they give of themselves, fill them with Your pleasure and our gratitude.

Reaching Beyond

☕ **Prayer Focus**–Governor

📖 **Scripture Inspiration**

Let every soul be subject to the governing authorities. For there is no authority except from God. (Romans 13:1 NKJV)

🌀 **Praying the Word**

Help me to submit to the office of the governor of our state, knowing that the authority to govern comes from You.

🌸 **Prayer Prompt**

Anoint our governor for the work You've called him to do. Grant him wisdom, and give Him Your vision for our state and the courage to see it become a reality.

Prayer Focus_____

Scripture Inspiration

_____

_____

Praying the Word

_____

_____

Prayer Prompt

_____

_____

_____

Prayer Focus_____

Scripture Inspiration

_____

_____

Praying the Word

_____

_____

Prayer Prompt

_____

_____

_____

Day 4

Praise

☕ **Prayer Focus**—Patience

📖 **Scripture Inspiration**

The Lord is not slow to fulfill his promise as some count slowness, but is patient toward you.
(2 Peter 3:9 ESV)

☺ **Praying the Word**

Lord, I know You will fulfill all Your promises in Your perfect timing. Help me to be patient, as You are patient toward me. I trust that any delay I perceive is in reality Your perfect wisdom being acted out on my behalf.

❀ **Prayer Prompt**

I'm so thankful that You are patient and longsuffering with me. I know that You have suffered with me a long time in some areas. Thank You for never giving up on me. I know that You will never leave me or forsake me. Thank You for believing in me and for Your willingness to wait patiently as I slowly become all that You've created me to be.

🍵 Prayer Focus _____

📖 Scripture Inspiration

_____
_____
_____
_____

☺ Praying the Word

_____
_____
_____
_____
_____
_____

🌸 Prayer Prompt

_____
_____
_____
_____
_____
_____
_____
_____
_____

Day 4

Self

☕ **Prayer Focus**—Marriage

📖 **Scripture Inspiration**

For this reason a man shall leave his father and mother and be joined to his wife, and the two shall become one flesh. This is a great mystery, but I speak concerning Christ and the church. (Ephesians 5:31–32 NKJV)

☉ **Praying the Word**

O Creator, enable my husband and me to cling to one another so completely that we are no longer acting as two separate people but as one married couple. As I respectfully submit to my husband and he sacrificially loves me, may the world see Christ's redemption plan through us.

🌸 **Prayer Prompt**

Thank You for my marriage—the good, the bad, and the ugly. Continue to refine me and change me through the hard times so that I might look and act more like You. Please bless our marriage and draw us each closer to You and, as a result, closer to each other. Keep us together, and do not let anything separate us. By Your grace make our marriage stronger every day.

🍵 Prayer Focus _____

📖 Scripture Inspiration

_____

_____

_____

_____

☺ Praying the Word

_____

_____

_____

_____

_____

🌸 Prayer Prompt

_____

_____

_____

_____

_____

_____

_____

_____

_____

35

Day 4

Husband

☕ **Prayer Focus**—Role as Father

📖 **Scripture Inspiration**

For whom the Lord loves He corrects, just as a father the son in whom he delights. (Proverbs 3:12 NKJV)

⊚ **Praying the Word**

Fill my husband's heart with Your love. Wash over him with fresh joy at the privilege of being a parent. Allow any discipline to flow out of this joy and love.

🌸 **Prayer Prompt**

Encourage my husband as a father. Give him wisdom to lead us as a family. Supply him with all the patience, self-control, gentleness, and courage he needs to be a father in today's world. Work a godly respect for authority in our children's hearts and an unconditional, affectionate, firm love in his heart for them.

Prayer Focus_____

Scripture Inspiration

_____
_____
_____
_____

Praying the Word

_____
_____
_____
_____
_____

Prayer Prompt

_____
_____
_____
_____
_____
_____
_____
_____
_____

Day 4
Children

☕ **Prayer Focus**—Walk with God

📖**Scripture Inspiration**

I have no greater joy than to hear that my children walk in truth. (3 John 4 NKJV)

◎ **Praying the Word**

Dear Jesus, please give me the incomparable joy of knowing that my children are walking with You.

🌼 **Prayer Prompt**

Heavenly Father, instill in my children a love for worship, prayer, and Your Word at an early age. Establish patterns of devotion in them now that will carry through the rest of their lives. Teach them to walk in the Spirit, depend on Your strength, love You with all their hearts, hear Your voice, obey Your commands, and follow hard after You.

Prayer Focus _____

Scripture Inspiration

_____

_____

_____

_____

Praying the Word

_____

_____

_____

_____

_____

_____

Prayer Prompt

_____

_____

_____

_____

_____

_____

_____

_____

_____

_____

Day 4

Personal Influences

☕ **Prayer Focus**–Associate Pastor

📖 **Scripture Inspiration**
Jonathon said to David, "Whatever you say, I will do for you."
(1 Samuel 20:4 ESV)

◎ **Praying the Word**
Anoint our associate pastor to be the armor-bearer for our senior pastor. Give him a ready willingness to serve the vision You have for our church.

❀ **Prayer Prompt**
Reveal to our associate pastor the important role he plays in our church. Strengthen him to support our senior pastor. Remind us to encourage him, but when we fail, may Your smile of recognition be enough.

Reaching Beyond

☕ **Prayer Focus**–Presidential Advisors

📖 **Scripture Inspiration**
With counsel and wisdom Daniel answered Arioch, the captain of the king's guard. (Daniel 2:14 NKJV)

◎ **Praying the Word**
May the president's advisors offer wise counsel.

❀ **Prayer Prompt**
Surround the president with good men and women who will boldly counsel him with wisdom from You. May they serve our country by serving our president from a pure heart.

Prayer Focus _____

Scripture Inspiration

_____

_____

Praying the Word

_____

_____

Prayer Prompt

_____

_____

_____

Prayer Focus _____

Scripture Inspiration

_____

_____

Praying the Word

_____

_____

Prayer Prompt

_____

_____

_____

Day 5

Praise

🍵 **Prayer Focus**—Holy Spirit

📖 **Scripture Inspiration**

But the Helper, the Holy Spirit, whom the Father will send in my name, he will teach you all things and bring to your remembrance all that I have said to you. (John 14:26 ESV)

◎ **Praying the Word**

Thank You, Father, for sending the Helper, the Holy Spirit, to teach me all things and remind me of everything You have said to me.

🌸 **Prayer Prompt**

I love the Holy Spirit; thank You for leaving Him here on earth when You went back to heaven. Father, fill me to overflowing with the Holy Spirit, and reveal Jesus to me and through me by His power. I worship You, God the Father, Son, and Holy Spirit.

🍵 Prayer Focus _____

📖 Scripture Inspiration

_____
_____
_____
_____

🌀 Praying the Word

_____
_____
_____
_____
_____
_____

🌸 Prayer Prompt

_____
_____
_____
_____
_____
_____
_____
_____
_____
_____

Day 5
Self

☕ **Prayer Focus**—Words

📖 Scripture Inspiration

Death and life are in the power of the tongue, and those who love it will eat its fruits. (Proverbs 18:21 ESV)

☉ Praying the Word

I am aware of the destruction my own tongue can bring and also its power to bring life. My desire is that my words be sweet and satisfying and that they bring health to all those who hear them.

🌸 Prayer Prompt

I realize that any word that comes out of my mouth originates in my heart. With that in mind, I ask You to cleanse me from within and fill me with Your Spirit so that I may speak words that bring life. Most of all, may my words be pleasing to You.

🍵 Prayer Focus _____

📖 Scripture Inspiration

_____

_____

_____

_____

☉ Praying the Word

_____

_____

_____

_____

_____

🐝 Prayer Prompt

_____

_____

_____

_____

_____

_____

_____

_____

_____

Day 5
Husband

☕ **Prayer Focus**—Work

📖 **Scripture Inspiration**

Let the favor of the Lord our God be upon us, and establish the work of our hands upon us; yes, establish the work of our hands! (Psalm 90:17 ESV)

☺ **Praying the Word**

God, I pray that not only would Your favor be upon my husband, but that he would also be well-regarded by all those he works for and with. I ask that everything he sets his hand toward would grow and multiply and that he would gain acceptance and recognition for the work You accomplish through him.

🌸 **Prayer Prompt**

I pronounce blessing on my husband's work. I'm asking for provision and favor in every area of his career. Give him a fresh joy for the place You've called him to minister and the work You've ordained for him to do. Give him wisdom and strength to do an excellent job with all of his heart. Remind him that he is ultimately working as unto You, not man.

Prayer Focus _____

Scripture Inspiration

_____
_____
_____
_____

Praying the Word

_____
_____
_____
_____
_____
_____

Prayer Prompt

_____
_____
_____
_____
_____
_____
_____
_____
_____

Day 5
Children

📖 **Scripture Inspiration**

Children, obey your parents in the Lord, for this is right.
(Ephesians 6:1 ESV)

⊙ **Praying the Word**

Lord, teach my children to love righteousness and, out of obedience to You, obey their parents.

🌼 **Prayer Prompt**

Please put a love for obedience in my children's hearts. May they long to do right and feel remorseful when they do wrong. Help me to train them to obey their father and me as their parents so they will follow You without arguing when they are grown. I pray they will develop a habit of complete obedience that comes from a heart that trusts Your Word and wants to please You.

🍵 Prayer Focus _____

📖 Scripture Inspiration

_____

_____

_____

_____

🌀 Praying the Word

_____

_____

_____

_____

_____

_____

🌸 Prayer Prompt

_____

_____

_____

_____

_____

_____

_____

_____

_____

_____

Day 5

Personal Influences

☕ **Prayer Focus**–Church

📖 **Scripture Inspiration**

So the churches were strengthened in the faith, and they increased in numbers daily. (Acts 16:5 ESV)

🕓 **Praying the Word**

Build up our church in strong relationships with You and each other and out of that strength draw many people to You.

❀ **Prayer Prompt**

Keep our church living and breathing Your Spirit so there may be unity and vision within the body. Cover all the details that are part of running an organization, and make our church a light to our community.

Reaching Beyond

☕ **Prayer Focus**–Local Government

📖 **Scripture Inspiration**

Choose some men from each tribe who have wisdom, understanding, and a good reputation. (Deuteronomy 1:13 NLT)

🕓 **Praying the Word**

Help us to perceive Your will when we vote. May we choose wise, understanding men and women with good reputations.

❀ **Prayer Prompt**

Help us take our privilege to vote seriously by researching the candidates and issues so we can use our influence for righteousness.

☕ Prayer Focus_____

📖 Scripture Inspiration

_____

_____

☾ Praying the Word

_____

_____

❀ Prayer Prompt

_____

_____

_____

☕ Prayer Focus_____

📖 Scripture Inspiration

_____

_____

☾ Praying the Word

_____

_____

❀ Prayer Prompt

_____

_____

_____

Day 6

Praise

☕ **Prayer Focus**—Forgiveness

📖 **Scripture Inspiration**

You answered them, O Lord our God; You were to them God-Who-Forgives. (Psalm 99:8 NKJV)

ⓒ **Praying the Word**

You have answered me, O Lord, my God of Forgiveness, which is Your very name and character.

🌸 **Prayer Prompt**

How can I even begin to thank You for Your forgiveness? Without the sacrifice of Your Son, Jesus, I would be so lost and eaten up with guilt. I am eternally grateful for, not only the forgiveness of my sins, but also Your ongoing forgiveness of my weaknesses and selfishness. Thank You, too, for choosing to forget my sin. I receive the free gift of forgiveness that You give.

☕ Prayer Focus_____

📖 Scripture Inspiration

_____
_____
_____
_____

◎ Praying the Word

_____
_____
_____
_____
_____

🌸 Prayer Prompt

_____
_____
_____
_____
_____
_____
_____
_____
_____

Day 6

Self

☕ **Prayer Focus**—Thoughts

📖Scripture Inspiration

Do not be conformed to this world, but be transformed by the renewal of your mind. (Romans 12:2 ESV)

☺ Praying the Word

I do not want to become like the world, and I know that any change begins with my thoughts. Cleanse my mind, and help me to focus on You so that I might become like You.

🌸 Prayer Prompt

Help me to bring every thought into captivity to the obedience of Christ. When my mind starts to wander down paths that eventually lead to sin, stop me in my tracks so that I might repent and turn around to walk toward You. Remind me to meditate on Your Word when I'm tempted to dwell on negative or sinful thoughts.

☕ Prayer Focus_____

📖 Scripture Inspiration

_____
_____
_____
_____

◎ Praying the Word

_____
_____
_____
_____
_____

❀ Prayer Prompt

_____
_____
_____
_____
_____
_____
_____
_____

Day 6
Husband

☕ **Prayer Focus**—Finances

📖Scripture Inspiration

Be diligent to know the state of your flocks, and attend to your herds, for riches are not forever, nor does a crown endure for all generations. (Proverbs 27: 23–24 NKJV)

☺ Praying the Word

Bolster my husband's resolve to pay diligent attention to our finances. Motivate him to look down the road and be ready for the future. Give him wisdom to attend to our future.

🌸 Prayer Prompt

Lord, give us peace when it comes to finances. Teach us how to live comfortably with everything You have provided for us. Keep us from spending more than we need, so that stress and division can't find a place within our home. Increase our faith to remember that You are willing and able to supply all of our needs. Thank You for the privilege of giving a portion back to You in tithes and offerings.

Prayer Focus_____

Scripture Inspiration

_____
_____
_____
_____

Praying the Word

_____
_____
_____
_____
_____

Prayer Prompt

_____
_____
_____
_____
_____
_____
_____
_____
_____

Day 6
Children

☕ **Prayer Focus**—Holiness

📖 **Scripture Inspiration**

As He who called you is holy, you also be holy in all your conduct, since it is written, "You shall be holy, for I am holy." (1 Peter 1: 15–16 ESV)

☺ **Praying the Word**

O Holy Lord, because You have called my children unto holiness, I ask You to give them the power to walk in holiness.

❀ **Prayer Prompt**

Almighty God, I consecrate my children to You and ask that You would set them apart for Your holy purposes. May they love the things that You love and hate the things that You hate. Teach them to run from the kingdom of this world and walk in the kingdom of heaven.

Prayer Focus _____

Scripture Inspiration

_____

_____

_____

_____

Praying the Word

_____

_____

_____

_____

_____

_____

Prayer Prompt

_____

_____

_____

_____

_____

_____

_____

_____

_____

_____

Day 6

Personal Influences

☕ **Prayer Focus**–Friends

📖 **Scripture Inspiration**
As iron sharpens iron, a friend sharpens a friend.
(Proverbs 27:17 NLT)

☉ **Praying the Word**
Make me the kind of friend who draws others closer to You and challenges them to be more like Jesus by my example.

❀ **Prayer Prompt**
Bless my friends and their families. Show me ways to touch their lives with a word, favor, hug, or prayer. Bring younger women into my life that I can disciple and mentors from whom I can learn.

Reaching Beyond

☕ **Prayer Focus**–Supreme Court

📖 **Scripture Inspiration**
You shall not show partiality in judgment; . . . you shall not be afraid in any man's presence, for the judgment is God's.
(Deuteronomy 1:17 NKJV)

☉ **Praying the Word**
Enable the justices of the Supreme Court to judge without prejudice and to fear only You.

❀ **Prayer Prompt**
I lift up all members of the court systems and ask You to guide them with wisdom and a clear conscience.

Prayer Focus_____

Scripture Inspiration

_____

_____

Praying the Word

_____

_____

Prayer Prompt

_____

_____

_____

Prayer Focus_____

Scripture Inspiration

_____

_____

Praying the Word

_____

_____

Prayer Prompt

_____

_____

_____

Day 7

Praise

Prayer Focus—Love

Scripture Inspiration

So we have come to know and to believe the love that God has for us. God is love, and whoever abides in love abides in God, and God abides in him. (1 John 4:16 ESV)

Praying the Word

God, I believe the love that You have for me; help me to come to know it in greater measure every day. You are love. Enable me to rest and wait so completely in Your love that I do not look to anything or anyone else to satisfy me. I want to be found wholly in You and You holy in me.

Prayer Prompt

I praise You, O God of Love. It is because of Your love for us that You gave the gift of Love. Your love never changes; it is the same yesterday, today, and forever. Thank You that there is nothing I can do to make You love me any less and nothing I can do to make You love me any more. Love begins and ends in You.

Prayer Focus _____

Scripture Inspiration

_____

_____

_____

_____

Praying the Word

_____

_____

_____

_____

_____

_____

Prayer Prompt

_____

_____

_____

_____

_____

_____

_____

_____

_____

Day 7
Self

☕ **Prayer Focus**—Prayer Life

📖 Scripture Inspiration

Do not be anxious about anything, but in everything by prayer and supplication with thanksgiving let your requests be made known to God. (Philippians 4:6 ESV)

☺ Praying the Word

Dear God, I bring to You all of my concerns and needs. I thank You that You hear me and that You will answer me according to Your perfect will. Now that my desires are in Your hands, I won't worry about a thing.

🌸 Prayer Prompt

It is impossible to have a relationship without communication. My deepest desire is to know You as I am known by You. Draw me closer and closer to You through intimate conversation. Help me to remember that You desire relationship with me above anything I could ever do for You.

Prayer Focus_____

Scripture Inspiration

_____
_____
_____
_____

Praying the Word

_____
_____
_____
_____
_____
_____

Prayer Prompt

_____
_____
_____
_____
_____
_____
_____
_____
_____

Day 7
Husband

☕ **Prayer Focus**—Personal Walk

📖 **Scripture Inspiration**

Walk in a manner worthy of the calling to which you have been called, with all humility and gentleness, with patience, bearing with one another in love. (Ephesians 4:1–2 ESV)

☉ **Praying the Word**

Wherever my husband goes and whatever he does, may he remember that he is a living testimony for You. Remind him that by Your mercy, You have forgiven his sins so that he will desire to walk in humility and gentleness; with patience; being quick to understand, forgive, and love everyone he encounters.

🌿 **Prayer Prompt**

I pray that everything my husband thinks, says, and does will glorify You. Enable him to follow through on the heart commitment he has made to You. Encourage him to be quick to confess and repent when he strays from Your path. Give him a longing for integrity in the inner man that manifests itself in a holy walk before others.

Prayer Focus _____

📖 Scripture Inspiration

_____

_____

_____

_____

◎ Praying the Word

_____

_____

_____

_____

_____

🌼 Prayer Prompt

_____

_____

_____

_____

_____

_____

_____

_____

_____

67

Day 7
Children

☕ **Prayer Focus**—Purity

📖 **Scripture Inspiration**

For this is the will of God, your sanctification: that you abstain from sexual immorality; that each one of you know how to control his own body in holiness and honor, not in the passion of lust. (1 Thessalonians 4:3–5 ESV)

☺ **Praying the Word**

Dear God, I pray that my children will walk in Your will, with lives dedicated to Your holy ways. Give them the power to honor their bodies, keep themselves sexually pure, and the ability to control the lusts of the flesh.

❀ **Prayer Prompt**

Dear Lord, it takes supernatural power for children to remain sexually pure until marriage in today's world. So that is what I'm praying for on behalf of my children. Help them to remain in holiness and to resist the temptation to see how close to the edge they can go without falling. Remind them to use the sword of the Spirit as they hide Your word in their hearts and keep their thoughts pure as the first line of defense.

☕ Prayer Focus _____

📖 Scripture Inspiration

_____
_____
_____
_____

☺ Praying the Word

_____
_____
_____
_____
_____

🌸 Prayer Prompt

_____
_____
_____
_____
_____
_____
_____
_____
_____
_____

Day 7
Personal Influences

☕ **Prayer Focus**–Extended Family

📖 **Scripture Inspiration**
And they said, "Believe in the Lord Jesus, and you will be saved, you and your household." (Acts 16:31 ESV)

🜨 **Praying the Word**
I believe You, Jesus, as my Lord and Savior. Use me to reach every member of my family.

🌸 **Prayer Prompt**
Thank You for my family. I lift up my grandparents, parents, sisters, brothers, aunts, uncles, cousins, nieces, nephews—every relative in my family—and ask that You draw them close to You. Bless them and keep them until the day of Your return.

Reaching Beyond

☕ **Prayer Focus**–Public Schools

📖 **Scripture Inspiration**
Give instruction to a wise man, and he will be still wiser; teach a righteous man, and he will increase in learning.
(Proverbs 9:9 ESV)

🜨 **Praying the Word**
Make our children wise and righteous so they will love learning and grow in understanding and knowledge.

🌸 **Prayer Prompt**
Raise up godly teachers to penetrate our schools to instruct the next generation in wisdom and righteousness.

☕ Prayer Focus _____

📖 Scripture Inspiration

_____

_____

☉ Praying the Word

_____

_____

✤ Prayer Prompt

_____

_____

_____

☕ Prayer Focus _____

📖 Scripture Inspiration

_____

_____

☉ Praying the Word

_____

_____

✤ Prayer Prompt

_____

_____

_____

Day 8

Praise

☕ **Prayer Focus**—Calvary

📖 **Scripture Inspiration**

But God forbid that I should boast except in the cross of our Lord Jesus Christ, by whom the world has been crucified to me, and I to the world. (Galatians 6:14 NKJV)

⊚ **Praying the Word**

Dear God, don't let me even think of taking credit for anything that is good in me. If there be any good, it is only by the grace of my Lord Jesus Christ and the power in His blood that was shed for my sins on the cross. The world no longer has power over me. I choose to die to anything the world has to offer.

❀ **Prayer Prompt**

Worthy is the Lamb who was slain to receive power and riches and wisdom and strength and honor and glory and blessing! My life began here on earth when Your life ended here on earth. Thank You for walking that painful, humiliating, unfair road to Calvary and for willingly suffering on the cross so that I might experience the abundant life You have given me.

Prayer Focus_____

Scripture Inspiration

_____
_____
_____
_____

Praying the Word

_____
_____
_____
_____
_____
_____

Prayer Prompt

_____
_____
_____
_____
_____
_____
_____
_____
_____
_____

73

Day 8

Self

☕ **Prayer Focus**—Bible Study

📖 Scripture Inspiration

Open my eyes, that I may see wondrous things from Your Law. (Psalm 119:18 NKJV)

☉ Praying the Word

Reveal to me the secret treasures that are hidden in Your Word, O Lord.

❀ Prayer Prompt

I love Your law! Feed my soul as I feast on Your Word. Give me a fresh hunger to devour the Scriptures so that I am not satisfied unless I have been filled with Your truth every day. As I read, hide Your Word in my heart that I might not sin against You.

Prayer Focus _____

Scripture Inspiration

_____

_____

_____

_____

Praying the Word

_____

_____

_____

_____

_____

_____

Prayer Prompt

_____

_____

_____

_____

_____

_____

_____

_____

_____

Day 8
Husband

☕ **Prayer Focus**—Sexuality

📖 **Scripture Inspiration**

Let your fountain be blessed, and rejoice with the wife of your youth. As a loving deer and a graceful doe, let her breasts satisfy you at all times; and always be enraptured with her love. (Proverbs 5:18–19 NKJV)

☺ **Praying the Word**

Dear Creator, may the very life-giving source of my husband be blessed. Give us fresh enjoyment of each other and intimacy that reminds us of our first times when our love-making was full of wonder and excitement. May I be beautiful and vulnerable in my husband's eyes, and allow me to please him so completely that he is wholly satisfied with my love.

🌸 **Prayer Prompt**

Fortify my husband in the inner man that he might have the supernatural power to fight the lusts of the world that bombard him every day. Where there has been any history of brokenness or sin in the area of his sexuality, restore him to purity and wholeness. Bless our times of intimacy so that we become so completely one that neither the enemy nor the world nor man or woman can come between us.

Prayer Focus _____

Scripture Inspiration

_____
_____
_____
_____

Praying the Word

_____
_____
_____
_____
_____

Prayer Prompt

_____
_____
_____
_____
_____
_____
_____
_____
_____
_____

Day 8
Children

☕ **Prayer Focus**—Self-Control

📖 **Scripture Inspiration**

If you live according to the flesh you will die; but if by the Spirit you put to death the deeds of the body, you will live. (Romans 8:13 ESV)

© **Praying the Word**

Fill my children with Your Holy Spirit so they will have the discipline to crucify the flesh and, subsequently, be raised to new life.

❀ **Prayer Prompt**

Dear heavenly Father, grow the fruit of the spirit: love, joy, peace, patience, kindness, goodness, faithfulness, gentleness, and especially, self-control in my children. Help them to walk in the Spirit, and enable them to control their tempers, tongues, passions, and behavior. Remind them to call on You for strength when their flesh is weak.

Prayer Focus

Scripture Inspiration

_____

_____

_____

_____

Praying the Word

_____

_____

_____

_____

_____

Prayer Prompt

_____

_____

_____

_____

_____

_____

_____

_____

_____

Day 8

Personal Influences

☕ **Prayer Focus**–Teachers

📖 **Scripture Inspiration**

A wise teacher's words spur students to action and emphasize important truths. (Ecclesiastes 12:11 NLT)

🔵 **Praying the Word**

Fill my children's teachers with Your creativity so they can engender excitement about learning and have the ability to express concepts with clarity.

🌼 **Prayer Prompt**

Thank You for those You have chosen to teach my children. Give them compassionate understanding, love for their job, strength for the task, and wisdom. Show me ways to support them as they fulfill the high calling of influencing so many young lives.

Reaching Beyond

☕ **Prayer Focus**–The Media

📖 **Scripture Inspiration**

See to it that no one takes you captive by philosophy and empty deceit . . . and not according to Christ. (Colossians 2:8 ESV)

🔵 **Praying the Word**

Deliver us from the spirit of this age, and set us apart from the ungodly influences of the prince of the air.

🌼 **Prayer Prompt**

Appoint godly men and women who will raise a standard of righteousness in the influential media.

Prayer Focus_____

Scripture Inspiration

_____

_____

Praying the Word

_____

_____

Prayer Prompt

_____

_____

_____

Prayer Focus_____

Scripture Inspiration

_____

_____

Praying the Word

_____

_____

Prayer Prompt

_____

_____

_____

Day 9

Praise

☕ **Prayer Focus**—Deliverer

📖 **Scripture Inspiration**

But I am poor and needy; yet the Lord thinks upon me. You are my help and my deliverer; do not delay, O my God. (Psalm 40:17 NKJV)

☺ Praying the Word

I am small in worth, and yet, the Lord God Almighty thinks about me! O God, hurry up; help me and deliver me. I need You.

❀ Prayer Prompt

O Jehovah, my rock, my fortress, and my deliverer! When I feel weak, You are my strength. I can't save myself, but You promise to rescue me. I feel the enemy closing in all around me, and I don't have the power to fight him anymore. All I need to do is speak the mighty name of Jesus and trust You to unleash Your authority on my behalf. Thank You for being my deliverer.

☕ Prayer Focus_____

📖 Scripture Inspiration

_____
_____
_____
_____

🌀 Praying the Word

_____
_____
_____
_____
_____
_____

🌸 Prayer Prompt

_____
_____
_____
_____
_____
_____
_____
_____
_____

Day 9

Self

🍵 **Prayer Focus**—Confession and Repentance

📖 Scripture Inspiration

If we confess our sins, he is faithful and just to forgive us our sins and to cleanse us from all unrighteousness. For godly grief produces a repentance that leads to salvation without regret. (1 John 1:9; 2 Corinthians 7:10 ESV)

⊙ Praying the Word

I want to bring my sin into the light because I am assured that You will forgive me and cleanse me completely. I am sincerely sorry for choosing my way over Yours. Help me to return to life in You.

🌿 Prayer Prompt

I don't want to keep any sinful thought or deed hidden anymore. I confess my sin to You now, and I refuse to make any excuses for my choices. Please forgive me for turning from Your way. I want to follow You again. Change me from within by the power of the risen Lord.

🍵 Prayer Focus _____

📖 Scripture Inspiration

_____
_____
_____
_____

🌀 Praying the Word

_____
_____
_____
_____
_____
_____

🌸 Prayer Prompt

_____
_____
_____
_____
_____
_____
_____
_____
_____
_____

Day 9

Husband

☕ **Prayer Focus**—Health

📖 **Scripture Inspiration**

I will restore health to you, and your wounds I will heal.
(Jeremiah 30:17 ESV)

☺ Praying the Word

Thank You for Your promise, Lord, that You will heal my
husband and give him good health.

🌸 Prayer Prompt

Standing on Your Word, I pray for health, strength, and a
long life for my husband. If there is any hidden infirmity,
You can see it, so heal that too. I ask for a special touch of
healing on his heart, both physically and emotionally. Take
sickness away from the midst of him, and keep disease
from him. Thank You that he will fulfill all the number of
days You have planned for him.

🍵 Prayer Focus _____

📖 Scripture Inspiration

_____
_____
_____
_____

⊚ Praying the Word

_____
_____
_____
_____
_____
_____

❀ Prayer Prompt

_____
_____
_____
_____
_____
_____
_____
_____
_____
_____

Day 9
Children

☕ **Prayer Focus**–School

📖 **Scripture Inspiration**

All your children shall be taught by the Lord, and great shall be the peace of your children. (Isaiah 54:13 ESV)

☺ **Praying the Word**

Teach my children, Lord, and thank You for the peace they will enjoy by following Your instruction.

🌸 **Prayer Prompt**

First of all, I pray that my children will learn from You and seek Your wisdom, Lord. Beyond that I ask that You will grant my children a love for learning. Give them the ability to understand the things they are being taught and remember them even beyond the tests. Teach them to organize their assignments and their time wisely. Help them to be respectful of those in authority and to find favor with their teachers and classmates.

Prayer Focus _____

Scripture Inspiration

_____
_____
_____
_____

Praying the Word

_____
_____
_____
_____
_____

Prayer Prompt

_____
_____
_____
_____
_____
_____
_____
_____
_____

Day 9

Personal Influences

☕ **Prayer Focus**–In-laws

📖 **Scripture Inspiration**
In you all the families of the earth shall be blessed.
(Genesis 12:3 ESV)

☺ **Praying the Word**
Dear God, please use me to bless every member of my husband's family.

🌸 **Prayer Prompt**
I am so grateful for the husband You have allowed me to marry. I understand that along with the blessing of marrying into his family came my responsibility to show love, mercy, forgiveness, hospitality, and Christ's character. Please help me to do that.

Reaching Beyond

☕ **Prayer Focus**–The Military

📖 **Scripture Inspiration**
The horse is made ready for the day of battle, but the victory belongs to the Lord. (Proverbs 21:31 ESV)

☺ **Praying the Word**
Prepare the military strength of our nation, but remind us to put our faith in You, the Commander of the Lord's army.

🌸 **Prayer Prompt**
Thank You for the many men and women who serve in our nation's military. Bless them and keep them. Wrap Your arms of protection around them and their families.

Prayer Focus _____

Scripture Inspiration

_____

_____

Praying the Word

_____

_____

Prayer Prompt

_____

_____

_____

Prayer Focus _____

Scripture Inspiration

_____

_____

Praying the Word

_____

_____

Prayer Prompt

_____

_____

_____

Day 10

Praise

☕ **Prayer Focus**—Heavenly Father

📖 **Scripture Inspiration**

For the Father Himself loves you, because you have loved Me and have believed that I came from God. (John 16:27 ESV)

◎ **Praying the Word**

I am amazed that You, the Father of all, love me because I love Your Son, and I believe with all my heart that He is the Son of God and was sent by You.

🌸 **Prayer Prompt**

Dear heavenly Father, I long to curl up in Your lap like a little girl, rest in Your strong arms, and lay my head upon Your chest where I can hear Your heart beating with Your love for me, Your precious child. Thank You for the privilege of calling You "Abba." I love You, Daddy.

☕ Prayer Focus_____

📖 Scripture Inspiration

_____
_____
_____
_____

☉ Praying the Word

_____
_____
_____
_____
_____
_____

🌸 Prayer Prompt

_____
_____
_____
_____
_____
_____
_____
_____
_____

Day 10
Self

Prayer Focus—Faith

Scripture Inspiration

Without faith it is impossible to please Him, for he who comes to God must believe that He is, and that He is a rewarder of those who diligently seek Him. (Hebrews 11:6 NASB)

Praying the Word

I come to You, believing that You are the Almighty, Living God. I want to seek You with all my heart because I know that You are a rewarder. The greatest reward I could receive is pleasing You; give me that kind of faith.

Prayer Prompt

I believe; help my unbelief. I humbly ask for the gift of faith that I might believe the promises You have made to me. Help me to so trust You that I begin thanking You in advance for answers to prayers that I cannot yet see. Increase my faith so that I can receive all that You have in store for me and the others I pray for.

Prayer Focus_____

Scripture Inspiration

_____

_____

_____

_____

Praying the Word

_____

_____

_____

_____

_____

Prayer Prompt

_____

_____

_____

_____

_____

_____

_____

_____

_____

Day 10
Husband

☕ **Prayer Focus**—Humility

📖 **Scripture Inspiration**

Let nothing be done through selfish ambition or conceit, but in lowliness of mind let each esteem others better than himself. (Philippians 2:3 NKJV)

☺ **Praying the Word**

Help my husband to serve others and even put them before himself. Keep him from selfishness or his own agenda or thinking more of himself than he should. Remind him of Your mercy toward him when he was yet a sinner.

🌸 **Prayer Prompt**

Open my husband's eyes to glimpse as much of Your glory as he can handle. May seeing You cause a natural humility and ongoing waves of worship. Remind him that anything that is praiseworthy in him comes from Your good hand. Teach him to enjoy walking in Your shadow.

☕ **Prayer Focus**_____

📖 Scripture Inspiration

_____
_____
_____
_____

🌀 Praying the Word

_____
_____
_____
_____
_____

🌸 Prayer Prompt

_____
_____
_____
_____
_____
_____
_____
_____

Day 10

Children

☕ **Prayer Focus**—Heart

📖 **Scripture Inspiration**

I will put My laws into their minds, and write them on their hearts, and I will be their God, and they shall be my people. (Hebrews 8:10 ESV)

☉ **Praying the Word**

Almighty God, I ask You to put Your laws in my children's minds and write them on their hearts. I pray they will make You their God and will be Your people.

🌸 **Prayer Prompt**

Father, my goal as a parent is that ultimately my children will love You and obey You from their hearts. As I train them from the outside-in, I ask You to shape and mold their hearts from the inside-out. I come against any legalism or obedience that is only for show. I pray that out of their hearts will flow rivers of living water. Thank You.

Prayer Focus _____

Scripture Inspiration

_____

_____

_____

_____

Praying the Word

_____

_____

_____

_____

_____

_____

Prayer Prompt

_____

_____

_____

_____

_____

_____

_____

_____

_____

_____

Day 10

Personal Influences

☕ **Prayer Focus**–Kids' Friends

📖 **Scripture Inspiration**
Do not be deceived: "Bad company ruins good morals."
(1 Corinthians 15:33 ESV)

☉ **Praying the Word**
Encourage each of my children's friends to make right choices so they can build each other up in their walk with You.

🌸 **Prayer Prompt**
Thank You for my children's friends. Keep each one safe, and help them grow in wisdom, stature, and in favor with You and man. Enable my children to be a good influence and a strong witness of the wisdom in following You.

Reaching Beyond

☕ **Prayer Focus**–The House and Senate

📖 **Scripture Inspiration**
You will live under a government that is just and fair. Your enemies will stay far away; you will live in peace. Terror will not come near. (Isaiah 54:14 NLT)

☉ **Praying the Word**
Make our government just and fair. Keep our enemies far away, hold back any threat of terrorism, and give us peace.

🌸 **Prayer Prompt**
Purge all politics from government, and instead, may we as a nation be driven by what is right and good in Your sight.

☕ Prayer Focus _____

📖 Scripture Inspiration

_____

_____

☾ Praying the Word

_____

_____

❀ Prayer Prompt

_____

_____

_____

☕ Prayer Focus _____

📖 Scripture Inspiration

_____

_____

☾ Praying the Word

_____

_____

❀ Prayer Prompt

_____

_____

_____

Praise

☕ **Prayer Focus**—Friend

📖 **Scripture Inspiration**

No longer do I call you servants, for the servant does not know what his master is doing; but I have called you friends, for all that I have heard from my Father I have made known to you. (John 15:15 ESV)

☺ **Praying the Word**

I cannot believe that the God of the universe calls me friend. Even if You, Jesus, no longer call me servant, I long to be Your servant. Help me to know You, Master, and Your purposes. Open my ears to hear everything You reveal to me from Your Father.

🌸 **Prayer Prompt**

It is beyond my imagination that You would want me as a friend, but I will accept Your mercy and gratefully welcome Your friendship. Thank You for walking beside me through the dailyness of my days. Sweet Jesus, You are that friend who sticks closer than a brother. I'm so happy to know that nothing can separate me from Your love.

Prayer Focus _____

Scripture Inspiration

_____

_____

_____

_____

Praying the Word

_____

_____

_____

_____

_____

Prayer Prompt

_____

_____

_____

_____

_____

_____

_____

_____

_____

Day 11

Self

☕ **Prayer Focus**—Ministry

📖Scripture Inspiration

Having gifts that differ according to the grace given to us, let us use them. (Romans 12:6 ESV)

☺ Praying the Word

Thank You for the specific gifts that You have given me by Your grace. Help me to use them for Your glory.

❀ Prayer Prompt

Anoint me to minister in ways and to those You have called me to serve. Keep me from coveting someone else's gifts, talents, or calling. Reveal to me the plans You have to use my gifts so that I may lay them at Your feet and be used by You according to Your will. May You be glorified through me.

Prayer Focus _____

Scripture Inspiration

_____
_____
_____
_____

Praying the Word

_____
_____
_____
_____
_____

Prayer Prompt

_____
_____
_____
_____
_____
_____
_____
_____
_____
_____

Day 11

Husband

☕ **Prayer Focus**—Protection

📖**Scripture Inspiration**

You have hedged me behind and before, and laid Your hand upon me. (Psalm 139:5 NKJV)

☺ Praying the Word

What peace to know that You have surrounded my husband with Your protection and that every aspect of his life is completely in Your trustworthy hand.

❀ Prayer Prompt

Thank You, Father, for protecting my husband, our household, and all that he has on every side. Put angels all around him to keep him from any accidents or injuries. Stand guard over his reputation or any traps the evil one may have set for him. I will rest today knowing that no weapon formed against him will prosper. He is safe in Your hands.

🍵 Prayer Focus _____

📖 Scripture Inspiration

_____
_____
_____
_____

🗺 Praying the Word

_____
_____
_____
_____
_____
_____

🌸 Prayer Prompt

_____
_____
_____
_____
_____
_____
_____
_____
_____
_____

Day 11
Children

📖 Scripture Inspiration

Whatever is true, whatever is honorable, whatever is just, whatever is pure, whatever is lovely, whatever is commendable, if there is any excellence, if there is anything worthy of praise, think about these things. (Philippians 4:8 ESV)

☺ Praying the Word

Sweet Lord, direct my children's thoughts to only dwell on things that are true, honorable, just, pure, lovely, commendable, excellent, and worthy of praise.

❀ Prayer Prompt

Heavenly Father, I can't read my children's minds, but You can. Would You please pay close attention to the things they are thinking and redirect their thoughts when they aren't pleasing to You? If they begin stuffing their feelings, harboring fear, sinking into depression, or believing lies, please bring these thoughts out into the open so we can bring them before Your healing Light of Truth. Fill their thoughts with Your love and life.

🍵 Prayer Focus _____

📖 Scripture Inspiration

_____
_____
_____
_____

© Praying the Word

_____
_____
_____
_____
_____
_____

🌸 Prayer Prompt

_____
_____
_____
_____
_____
_____
_____
_____
_____

Day 11

Personal Influences

☕ **Prayer Focus**–Kids' Friends' Parents

📖 **Scripture Inspiration**

Children, obey your parents in everything, for this pleases the Lord. (Colossians 3:20 ESV)

🕗 **Praying the Word**

Fortify the parents of my children's friends to require obedience in everything so they may know and enjoy Your pleasure.

🦋 **Prayer Prompt**

Lord, I know friends greatly influence my children. Please strengthen the homes of my children's friends. Because of a sure foundation at home, may my children and their friends find support from each other to stand firm in the midst of peer pressure.

Reaching Beyond

☕ **Prayer Focus**–Enemies

📖 **Scripture Inspiration**

I say to you, "Love your enemies and pray for those who persecute you." (Matthew 5:43 ESV)

🕗 **Praying the Word**

We obey Your commands as we pray for our enemies, and we ask You to reveal how we can show them Your love.

🦋 **Prayer Prompt**

Lord, I lift up those who have personally hurt me. I will to forgive them, and I give up my rights and requirements of restitution. I ask You to bless them.

Prayer Focus _____

Scripture Inspiration

_____
_____

Praying the Word

_____
_____

Prayer Prompt

_____
_____
_____

Prayer Focus _____

Scripture Inspiration

_____
_____

Praying the Word

_____
_____

Prayer Prompt

_____
_____
_____

Praise

☕ **Prayer Focus**—Counselor

📖 **Scripture Inspiration**

And His name shall be called Wonderful Counselor, Mighty God, Everlasting Father, Prince of Peace. (Isaiah 9:6 ESV)

☺ **Praying the Word**

Help me to know You, Lord, as the Wonderful Counselor, Mighty God, the Everlasting Father, and the Prince of Peace.

🌼 **Prayer Prompt**

The wisdom of the Creator of the galaxies has offered His counsel to me. I humbly bow before You and thank You for Your guidance. May I have a teachable spirit that I might honor every truth that You so graciously reveal to me. It is my fervent desire to seek Your will in every area of my life. I submit to Your counsel and worship You as Wonderful Counselor.

Prayer Focus _____

Scripture Inspiration

_____
_____
_____
_____

Praying the Word

_____
_____
_____
_____
_____
_____

Prayer Prompt

_____
_____
_____
_____
_____
_____
_____
_____
_____

113

Day 12
Self

☕ **Prayer Focus**—My Offspring

📖 **Scripture Inspiration**

In your offspring shall all the nations of the earth be blessed, because you have obeyed my voice. (Genesis 22:18 ESV)

☺ **Praying the Word**

Father God, help me to withhold nothing from You but to walk in complete trust and obedience. Thank You for the promise that You will bless the nations of the earth through my offspring.

🌸 **Prayer Prompt**

I know how earnestly I pray for my children because I love them so desperately. I can only imagine that I will certainly feel at least that strong of emotion and concern for my grandchildren. Because I believe that my love will increase exponentially with each generation, I pray in advance for salvation and abundant life for every child that will ultimately proceed from me until the return of Christ Jesus.

🍵 Prayer Focus_____

📖 Scripture Inspiration

_____

_____

_____

_____

🌀 Praying the Word

_____

_____

_____

_____

_____

🌸 Prayer Prompt

_____

_____

_____

_____

_____

_____

_____

_____

_____

_____

Day 12

Husband

☕ **Prayer Focus**—Integrity

📖 **Scripture Inspiration**

He who walks with integrity walks securely. (Proverbs 10:9 NKJV)

◎ **Praying the Word**

May my husband walk with a heart that is clean before You so that he has nothing to be afraid of.

🌸 **Prayer Prompt**

Prompt my husband to invite You into the secret places of his heart. Search his heart, and illuminate anything that is hiding in the shadows. May he so enjoy walking in the light as You are in the light that he would not tolerate even a hint of darkness. May he live his life before an audience of One.

Prayer Focus_____

Scripture Inspiration

_____
_____
_____
_____

Praying the Word

_____
_____
_____
_____
_____
_____

Prayer Prompt

_____
_____
_____
_____
_____
_____
_____
_____
_____
_____

Day 12
Children

☕ **Prayer Focus**—Words

📖 **Scripture Inspiration**

Let the words of my mouth and the meditation of my heart be acceptable in Your sight, O Lord, my strength and my redeemer. (Psalm 19:14 NKJV)

☺ **Praying the Word**

O Lord, redeem my children and be their strength. As You keep Your eyes upon them, let everything they think and say be acceptable to You.

❀ **Prayer Prompt**

Dear God, You are their Father, so help them to speak truth and not lies. Teach them to bridle their tongues, and strengthen their resolve not to fall into bad habits of coarse jesting, inappropriate humor, or profanity of any kind. May they cringe at the thought of hurting someone with their words. Instead, may they know the joy of speaking just the right word at the right time.

Prayer Focus _____

Scripture Inspiration

_____
_____
_____
_____

Praying the Word

_____
_____
_____
_____
_____
_____

Prayer Prompt

_____
_____
_____
_____
_____
_____
_____
_____
_____
_____

Day 12

Personal Influences

☕ **Prayer Focus**–Pets

📖 **Scripture Inspiration**
A righteous man regards the life of his animal.
(Proverbs 12:10 NKJV)

◎ **Praying the Word**
Lord, help our family to learn responsibility and grow in righteousness as we take good care of our pets.

🌸 **Prayer Prompt**
Thank You for the joy and unconditional love our pets give us. Help us give them the time and attention they need. Teach my children as they care for them, and help them make wonderful childhood memories. Please keep our pets safe and healthy.

Reaching Beyond

☕ **Prayer Focus**–Missionaries

📖 **Scripture Inspiration**
Pray earnestly to the Lord of the harvest to send out laborers into his harvest. (Matthew 9:37–38 ESV)

◎ **Praying the Word**
Raise up men and women who feel Your call on their lives to go into the world to preach the gospel of Jesus Christ.

🌸 **Prayer Prompt**
Comfort and strengthen all who are already laboring throughout the earth. Encourage their hearts, and pour out fresh anointing on them.

Prayer Focus _____

Scripture Inspiration

_____

_____

Praying the Word

_____

_____

Prayer Prompt

_____

_____

_____

Prayer Focus _____

Scripture Inspiration

_____

_____

Praying the Word

_____

_____

Prayer Prompt

_____

_____

_____

Day 13

Praise

☕ **Prayer Focus**—Healer

📖 **Scripture Inspiration**

And when Jesus went out He saw a great multitude; and He was moved with compassion for them, and healed their sick.
(Matthew 14:14 NKJV)

⊙ Praying the Word

Jesus, I know that even amidst the multitude, You see me. I believe that my needs touch Your heart and that You can heal me.

❀ Prayer Prompt

Jesus, You are the same yesterday, today, and forever. I am so grateful that You are still in the miracle-working business. I believe that by Your stripes I am healed, and I worship You as the Resurrection and the Life. O Keeper of the keys of death, I exalt You.

Prayer Focus _____

Scripture Inspiration

_____

_____

_____

_____

Praying the Word

_____

_____

_____

_____

_____

Prayer Prompt

_____

_____

_____

_____

_____

_____

_____

_____

_____

Day 13
Self

☕ **Prayer Focus**—Health

📖 **Scripture Inspiration**

Beloved, I pray that all may go well with you and that you may be in good health, as it goes well with your soul.
(3 John 2 ESV)

☉ **Praying the Word**

I receive the apostle John's prayers for myself that all may go well with me and that I may be healthy in body and soul.

🌸 **Prayer Prompt**

Jesus, as You walked the earth, You healed the sick and the brokenhearted. You also said if I asked, I would receive. So I'm asking that You would give me good health. Keep me from sickness and disease of the body, soul, or mind. Make me strong and healthy so that I can serve You diligently all the days of my life. Should You choose in Your wisdom and mercy to allow me to suffer, let it bring You glory.

Prayer Focus

Scripture Inspiration

_____

_____

_____

_____

Praying the Word

_____

_____

_____

_____

_____

Prayer Prompt

_____

_____

_____

_____

_____

_____

_____

_____

_____

Day 13
Husband

☕ **Prayer Focus**–Thought Life

📖 **Scripture Inspiration**

You keep him in perfect peace whose mind is stayed on you, because he trusts in you. (Isaiah 26:3 ESV)

◎ **Praying the Word**

Help my husband to keep his thoughts so focused on You and Your trustworthiness that he rests completely in Your plan for his life.

❀ **Prayer Prompt**

Train my husband to think about You, Your Word, and Your ways when he is tempted by the enemy in his thought life. Cleanse him from any impure, anxious, or deceiving thoughts, and strengthen him to hold fast to the Truth. Make him diligent to keep the door to his heart guarded as he takes every thought captive to the obedience of Christ.

🍵 Prayer Focus _____

📖 Scripture Inspiration

_____
_____
_____
_____

◎ Praying the Word

_____
_____
_____
_____
_____
_____

❀ Prayer Prompt

_____
_____
_____
_____
_____
_____
_____
_____
_____
_____

Day 13
Children

☕ **Prayer Focus**—Protection

📖 **Scripture Inspiration**

Pour out your heart like water before the face of the Lord. Lift your hands toward Him for the life of your young children. (Lamentations 2:19 NKJV)

⊙ **Praying the Word**

I come before You, Lord, and pour out my heart to You. I surrender my children to You and ask that You would keep and protect them all the days of their lives.

🌸 **Prayer Prompt**

Thankfully, I know that You love my dear children even more than I do. With that in mind, I hand them over to You. I am confident that You have given Your angels charge over my children and they will keep them in all their ways. Help me not to fear but to rest in Your ability to protect my children and to trust that the enemy will not be allowed to touch my children without Your permission. They are safe with You.

Prayer Focus _____

Scripture Inspiration

_____
_____
_____
_____

Praying the Word

_____
_____
_____
_____
_____

Prayer Prompt

_____
_____
_____
_____
_____
_____
_____
_____
_____

Day 13

Personal Influences

☕ **Prayer Focus**–Boss

📖 **Scripture Inspiration**
If the master returns and finds that the servant has done a good job, there will be a reward. (Matthew 24:46 NLT)

☉ **Praying the Word**
Lord, I pray that my husband's (and/or my) boss would be happy with the job being done, recognize integrity and hard work, and reward appropriately.

🌸 **Prayer Prompt**
Please bless my husband's (and/or my) boss. Give him grace to manage and wisdom to make good decisions. May his personal life and his business endeavors prosper. If he doesn't know You, open his eyes through my husband (and/or me.)

Reaching Beyond

☕ **Prayer Focus**–The Economy

📖 **Scripture Inspiration**
Your God will bless you . . . and you shall lend to many nations, but you shall not borrow. (Deuteronomy 16:6 ESV)

☉ **Praying the Word**
We stand on Your Word, believing that we are called to be a ruling nation that is rich in generosity and not in debt.

🌸 **Prayer Prompt**
May we as a nation spend wisely and with integrity. Create jobs so that everyone can provide for their own families. In mercy bless us, Lord.

☕ Prayer Focus _____

📖 Scripture Inspiration

_____

_____

✉ Praying the Word

_____

_____

✿ Prayer Prompt

_____

_____

_____

☕ Prayer Focus _____

📖 Scripture Inspiration

_____

_____

✉ Praying the Word

_____

_____

✿ Prayer Prompt

_____

_____

_____

Day 14

Praise

☕ **Prayer Focus**—Provider

📖**Scripture Inspiration**

If you then, being evil, know how to give good gifts to your children, how much more will your Father who is in heaven give good things to those who ask Him. (Matthew 7:11 NKJV)

☺ **Praying the Word**

Father, I know even I, as a sinful parent, love to give good gifts to my children. You, who own the storehouses of heaven, love to give good things to us as Your children even more! You are just waiting for us to ask. So, here's me asking.

🌸 **Prayer Prompt**

I will not worry about tomorrow because I know that You already have a plan to supply all of my needs according to Your riches in glory by Christ Jesus. Therefore, I praise You now for that which I cannot see, and by faith I will thank You in advance because I know You are trustworthy. Thank You for providing for my every need (and more wants than I should have). I am grateful to You, my generous Gift Giver.

Prayer Focus _____

Scripture Inspiration

_____
_____
_____
_____

Praying the Word

_____
_____
_____
_____
_____
_____

Prayer Prompt

_____
_____
_____
_____
_____
_____
_____
_____
_____
_____

Day 14
Self

☕ **Prayer Focus**—Relationships

📖Scripture Inspiration

Pursue peace with all people, and holiness, without which no one will see the Lord. (Hebrews 12:14 NKJV)

☺ Praying the Word

I pray that people will see You, Lord, through me as I strive to walk in holiness by Your Spirit working in me. Help me to be a peacemaker in all of my relationships.

✿ Prayer Prompt

Lord, would You please use me to touch the people in my life with Your love and life? I pray for peaceful relationships without strife or confusion. Give me the kind of "iron sharpens iron," "speak the truth in love," and "fellowship of the Spirit" friendships with other women.

🍵 Prayer Focus _____

📖 Scripture Inspiration

_____
_____
_____
_____

☯ Praying the Word

_____
_____
_____
_____
_____
_____

🌸 Prayer Prompt

_____
_____
_____
_____
_____
_____
_____
_____
_____
_____

Day 14
Husband

📖Scripture Inspiration

Let no corrupting talk come out of your mouths, but only such as is good for building up, as fits the occasion, that it may give grace to those who hear. (Ephesians 4:29 ESV)

☉ Praying the Word

Lord, I pray that every word my husband speaks would encourage, be appropriate, be honest, and would bless those around him.

❀ Prayer Prompt

Thank You for the gift of communication. Reveal to my husband the power he possesses to create life with his words. Help him understand how much I love to hear what he has to say and how his words affect me and the children. Teach him to guard his tongue from coarse talk, lies, criticism, broken promises, and words spoken in anger. May his words flow from a heart that loves Your Word.

🍵 Prayer Focus _____

📖 Scripture Inspiration

_____
_____
_____
_____

☺ Praying the Word

_____
_____
_____
_____
_____
_____

🌼 Prayer Prompt

_____
_____
_____
_____
_____
_____
_____
_____
_____

Day 14
Children

☕ **Prayer Focus**—Health

📖 **Scripture Inspiration**

Bless the Lord, O my soul, and forget not all his benefits,
who forgives all your iniquity and heals all your diseases.
(Psalm 103:2–3 ESV)

☺ **Praying the Word**

I bless You, Lord, with everything that's within me. Help my children never to forget all Your blessings toward them, especially the forgiveness of their sins. Thank You for the added blessing of Your power to heal them. I claim that now for my children.

🌸 **Prayer Prompt**

Father, I ask You to give my children good health. Strengthen their immune systems. Keep them from accidents. Any diseases that might try to rear their ugly heads, cover now with Your healing hand. Great Physician, should You decide to heal them through the blessing of medicine, lead us to the doctors You have chosen for them and anoint their hands with the power of Your touch.

Prayer Focus_____

Scripture Inspiration

_____
_____
_____
_____

Praying the Word

_____
_____
_____
_____
_____
_____

Prayer Prompt

_____
_____
_____
_____
_____
_____
_____
_____
_____
_____

Day 14

Personal Influences

☕ **Prayer Focus**–Coworkers

📖 **Scripture Inspiration**

You yourself must be an example to them by doing good deeds of every kind. Let everything you do reflect the integrity and seriousness of your teaching. (Titus 2:7 NLT)

🌀 **Praying the Word**

Allow my husband (and/or me) to be a good example to his/my coworkers. Let them see the character of Jesus in everything we do.

🌸 **Prayer Prompt**

Use my husband (and/or me) to draw coworkers to You. May they watch us and desire to know You personally. Bless their families, and give them fresh joy in their jobs. May peace reign throughout the company.

Reaching Beyond

☕ **Prayer Focus**–Jerusalem

📖 **Scripture Inspiration**

Pray for the peace of Jerusalem: "May they prosper who love you." (Psalm 122:6 NKJV)

🌀 **Praying the Word**

Dear God, we love Jerusalem, and we pray for the peace of Your holy city.

🌸 **Prayer Prompt**

Father, we ask for peace to reign in the Middle East and especially throughout Israel. Until Your return, hold back the killing and terrorizing of Your children.

☕ Prayer Focus _____

📖 Scripture Inspiration

_____

_____

☺ Praying the Word

_____

_____

✿ Prayer Prompt

_____

_____

_____

☕ Prayer Focus _____

📖 Scripture Inspiration

_____

_____

☺ Praying the Word

_____

_____

✿ Prayer Prompt

_____

_____

_____

Praise

☕ **Prayer Focus**—Peace

📖 **Scripture Inspiration**

Peace I leave with you; my peace I give to you. Not as the world gives do I give to you. Let not your hearts be troubled, neither let them be afraid. (John 14:27 ESV)

☺ **Praying the Word**

Lord Jesus, before You ascended to Your Father, You promised to leave Your peace with us. You have given me peace. Not the transitory kind the world offers, but lasting peace. Help me not to be anxious or afraid.

❀ **Prayer Prompt**

Thank You for the peace that passes understanding. I praise You for the supernatural calm that surrounds me, even in the midst of storms that rage around me. Speak "Peace, be still" to my heart when I begin to toss and turn in the tumult. You are my Prince of Peace, and I will trust in You.

Prayer Focus_____

Scripture Inspiration

_____
_____
_____
_____

Praying the Word

_____
_____
_____
_____
_____
_____

Prayer Prompt

_____
_____
_____
_____
_____
_____
_____
_____
_____
_____

Day 15
Self

☕ **Prayer Focus**–Diet

📖 **Scripture Inspiration**

So, whether you eat or drink, or whatever you do, do all to the glory of God. (1 Corinthians 10:31 ESV)

◎ **Praying the Word**

May everything that I eat or drink—and anything else I do, for that matter—always be a good witness of You.

❀ **Prayer Prompt**

I know that my body is the temple of the Holy Spirit. I desire to keep Your home strong, beautiful, and comfortable. Help me not to be as concerned about what the outside of Your house looks like as I am about the inside, where You live. Give me the self-discipline to eat foods that will keep my body well-built and long lasting.

Prayer Focus_____

Scripture Inspiration

_____

_____

_____

_____

Praying the Word

_____

_____

_____

_____

_____

Prayer Prompt

_____

_____

_____

_____

_____

_____

_____

_____

_____

Day 15
Husband

☕ **Prayer Focus**—Leader

📖 **Scripture Inspiration**

He must manage his own household well, with all dignity keeping his children submissive, for if someone does not know how to manage his own household, how will he care for God's church. (1 Timothy 3:4–5 ESV)

☺ **Praying the Word**

Anoint my husband to lead our family well. Because of his servant leadership, may he expect obedience from our children. Expand his influence to our church, and give him Your heart for those he leads in all arenas.

🌸 **Prayer Prompt**

Dear God, raise up my husband to be a strong commander in Your army. May he walk in Your authority wherever the sole of his foot trods. Give him a servant's heart and a leader's courage.

Prayer Focus _____

Scripture Inspiration

_____

_____

_____

_____

Praying the Word

_____

_____

_____

_____

_____

_____

Prayer Prompt

_____

_____

_____

_____

_____

_____

_____

_____

_____

Day 15
Children

☕ **Prayer Focus**—Gifts and Calling

📖 **Scripture Inspiration**

Having gifts that differ according to the grace given to us, let us use them. (Romans 12:6 ESV)

☺ Praying the Word

Thank You, Lord, that You give each of us in Your body different gifts. May my children be diligent to use the gifts You have so graciously given them to glorify You.

❀ Prayer Prompt

Heavenly Father, I ask You to reveal to my children at an early age the gifts You have given them and the calling and purpose for which You have created them. Keep them from looking in other directions so they don't waste time going down paths that will not ultimately be blessed or useful for Your kingdom. May they appreciate the gifts and enjoy the calling You have for them and never covet someone else's gifts or calling.

Prayer Focus_____

Scripture Inspiration

_____
_____
_____
_____

Praying the Word

_____
_____
_____
_____
_____
_____

Prayer Prompt

_____
_____
_____
_____
_____
_____
_____
_____
_____

Day 15

Personal Influences

☕ **Prayer Focus**–Neighbors

📖 **Scripture Inspiration**

Better is a neighbor who is near than a brother who is far away. (Proverbs 27:10 ESV)

◎ **Praying the Word**

Thank You for the gift of close neighbors. May our neighborhood be like a family as we reach out to serve one another.

🌸 **Prayer Prompt**

May Your spirit reign over our neighborhood and Your light shine from house to house. Place angels as guards over our homes and families, and use my hands to touch my neighbors with Your love.

Reaching Beyond

☕ **Prayer Focus**–The Poor and Defenseless

📖 **Scripture Inspiration**

Defend the poor and fatherless; do justice to the afflicted and needy. (Psalm 82:3 NKJV)

◎ **Praying the Word**

Lord, we lift up those who are living in poverty and without fathers. Help us to reach out to those in need.

🌸 **Prayer Prompt**

Father, You see all of the world's broken hearts. Reach down with Your tender mercy and allow each one of them to sense Your love and plan for their lives.

☕ Prayer Focus _____

📖 Scripture Inspiration

_____

_____

☉ Praying the Word

_____

_____

✿ Prayer Prompt

_____

_____

_____

☕ Prayer Focus _____

📖 Scripture Inspiration

_____

_____

☉ Praying the Word

_____

_____

✿ Prayer Prompt

_____

_____

_____

Day 16

Praise

☕ **Prayer Focus**—Comforter

📖 **Scripture Inspiration**

And I will pray the Father, and he shall give you another Comforter, that he may be with you for ever. (John 14:16 ASV)

☉ **Praying the Word**

Dear Father, thank You for giving me the Comforter. I know there is nothing I can go through that He will not be right beside me, even inside me.

❀ **Prayer Prompt**

Thank You for caring enough about my feelings that You specifically sent the Comforter to wrap Your arms around me when I am sad, disappointed, or afraid. I am grateful for Your presence that surrounds, consoles, and covers me.

🍵 Prayer Focus _____

📖 Scripture Inspiration

_____
_____
_____
_____

🌀 Praying the Word

_____
_____
_____
_____
_____
_____

🌸 Prayer Prompt

_____
_____
_____
_____
_____
_____
_____
_____
_____

Day 16

Self

☕ **Prayer Focus**—Exercise

📖 Scripture Inspiration

But I discipline my body and keep it under control.
(1 Corinthians 9:27 ESV)

☺ Praying the Word

Give me the strength to submit my flesh to the control of
Your Spirit.

❀ Prayer Prompt

Help me to take good care of this earthen vessel through
which You have chosen to fill and demonstrate Your excellent power. Strengthen me to make daily exercise some
kind of priority so I can keep my heart and body strong.
Allow me to feel the exhilaration that comes from exercise,
and may it lift my spirits, clear my mind, and boost my
energy for the tasks You've given me.

Prayer Focus_____

Scripture Inspiration

_____
_____
_____
_____

Praying the Word

_____
_____
_____
_____
_____

Prayer Prompt

_____
_____
_____
_____
_____
_____
_____
_____
_____

Day 16

Husband

☕ **Prayer Focus**—Self-Control

📖 **Scripture Inspiration**

A man without self-control is like a city broken into and left without walls. (Proverbs 25:28 ESV)

☺ Praying the Word

Dear Lord, guard and protect my husband by strengthening him with self-control.

❀ Prayer Prompt

Give my husband ability to walk in the spirit and not in the flesh. Keep him from angry outbursts, lustful indulgences, foolish impulses, harmful addictions, and careless words. Show him the power in a man who has learned to call out to You in his times of weakness. When he stumbles may he be quick to repent and reach up for Your hand to stand again.

Prayer Focus _____

Scripture Inspiration

_____
_____
_____
_____

Praying the Word

_____
_____
_____
_____
_____
_____

Prayer Prompt

_____
_____
_____
_____
_____
_____
_____
_____
_____
_____

Day 16
Children

☕ **Prayer Focus**—Repentance

📖 **Scripture Inspiration**

He who covers his sins will not prosper, but whoever confesses and forsakes them will have mercy. (Proverbs 28:13 NKJV)

⊙ **Praying the Word**

Teach my children the wisdom and freedom in confessing their sins and the power available to walk away from them. May they trust Your mercy and not be tempted to hide their sins, which leads to destruction.

🌸 **Prayer Prompt**

One of the most important things I want to ask for my children is that they know and love mercy. Reveal Your love for them so completely that they immediately confess their sin and repent because they can't stand even a moment's separation from You. May they boldly approach the throne of grace to receive strength not to sin again.

158

☕ Prayer Focus _____

📖 Scripture Inspiration

_____
_____
_____
_____

◉ Praying the Word

_____
_____
_____
_____
_____
_____

❀ Prayer Prompt

_____
_____
_____
_____
_____
_____
_____
_____
_____

Day 16
Personal Influences

☕ **Prayer Focus**–Unsaved Friends

📖 **Scripture Inspiration**
No one can come to me unless the Father who sent me draws him.
(John 6:44 ESV)

☉ **Praying the Word**
Dear Heavenly Father, I ask You to draw _____ into
a personal relationship with Jesus by Your Holy Spirit.

🌸 **Prayer Prompt**
Please bring people into my life who don't know You so that I
may have the privilege of sharing You through my life. Give me
opportunities, words, and courage to tell them about Your plan of
salvation, forgiveness, and hope for their lives.

Reaching Beyond

☕ **Prayer Focus**–Crime/Terrorism

📖 **Scripture Inspiration**
*Do not be afraid of sudden terror, nor of trouble from the wicked
when it comes; for the Lord will be your confidence.* (Proverbs
3:25–26 NKJV)

☉ **Praying the Word**
Thank You for Your protection and Your promise to keep us from
trouble and the plans of the wicked.

🌸 **Prayer Prompt**
We call upon You, Almighty God, to be our defender, fortress,
and strong tower. We will run to You and be safe.

Prayer Focus _____

Scripture Inspiration

_____

_____

Praying the Word

_____

_____

Prayer Prompt

_____

_____

_____

Prayer Focus _____

Scripture Inspiration

_____

_____

Praying the Word

_____

_____

Prayer Prompt

_____

_____

_____

Praise

Prayer Focus—Blood

Scripture Inspiration

But now in Christ Jesus you who once were far off have been brought near by the blood of Christ. (Ephesians 2:13 ESV)

Praying the Word

Because of the blood You shed on the cross for me, Christ Jesus, I who was so far away have now been brought near to You.

Prayer Prompt

O the blood of Jesus, that washes white as snow! Praise You, sweet Lamb of God, for the forgiveness, cleansing, and power that is in Your blood. Thank You that by it I may enter into the very Holy of Holies and be changed in the presence of God.

Prayer Focus_____

Scripture Inspiration

_____
_____
_____
_____

Praying the Word

_____
_____
_____
_____
_____

Prayer Prompt

_____
_____
_____
_____
_____
_____
_____
_____
_____
_____

Day 17

Self

☕ **Prayer Focus**—Obedience

📖 **Scripture Inspiration**

If you love me, obey my commandments. (John 14:15 NLT)

☺ **Praying the Word**

I do love You; help me to obey You.

❀ **Prayer Prompt**

I trust You, Lord. I know that anything You require of me is
for my own good. I choose to obey You rather than myself or
following after what others think I should do. I know there
is safety, protection, and blessing in obeying Your commands. Help me to be quicker and quicker to obey You and
show my deep love for You.

Prayer Focus_____

Scripture Inspiration

_____

_____

_____

_____

Praying the Word

_____

_____

_____

_____

_____

Prayer Prompt

_____

_____

_____

_____

_____

_____

_____

_____

_____

Day 17
Husband

☕ **Prayer Focus**—Wisdom

📖 **Scripture Inspiration**

A wise man will hear and increase learning, and a man of understanding will attain wise counsel. (Proverbs 1:5 NKJV)

☉ **Praying the Word**

Teach my husband to seek wise counsel, to hear it, understand it, and grow from it.

❀ **Prayer Prompt**

You are the Wonderful Counselor. May my husband always seek You first when he is looking for wisdom. Surround him, also, with godly friends and role models who will speak the truth in love. Put an insatiable desire for wisdom in his heart that will perpetually keep him seeking after You. Thank You for Your promise to give wisdom to all who ask. Encourage my husband to be a seeker and an asker.

🍵 Prayer Focus _____

📖 Scripture Inspiration

_____
_____
_____
_____

⑥ Praying the Word

_____
_____
_____
_____
_____
_____

🌸 Prayer Prompt

_____
_____
_____
_____
_____
_____
_____
_____
_____

Day 17
Children

☕ **Prayer Focus**—Friends

📖 **Scripture Inspiration**

Whoever walks with the wise becomes wise, but the companion of fools will suffer harm. (Proverbs 13:20 ESV)

🌀 **Praying the Word**

Show my children the wisdom of walking with those who fear and respect You. Help them to see that even if they walk in righteousness, they can still suffer the collateral damage of hanging out with fools.

🌸 **Prayer Prompt**

I am aware of how important my children's friends can be in their lives. I earnestly come to You and ask You to handpick the friends my children will have in every season of their lives. I take the authority that You have given me as their parent to draw a blood line around them to protect them from any unholy influences. Give them loyal, kind, wise, and godly friendships that will grow deeper as they grow older.

🍵 Prayer Focus_____

📖 Scripture Inspiration

_____
_____
_____
_____

☺ Praying the Word

_____
_____
_____
_____
_____

✿ Prayer Prompt

_____
_____
_____
_____
_____
_____
_____
_____
_____

Day 17

Personal Influences

☕ **Prayer Focus**–Sick Friends

📖 **Scripture Inspiration**

Is anyone among you sick? Let him call for the elders of the church, and let them pray over him, anointing him with oil in the name of the Lord. (James 5:14 ESV)

🕑 **Praying the Word**

Lord, I lift up my friend _____ and ask You to touch her by Your Spirit and bring healing in the name of Jesus.

🌸 **Prayer Prompt**

Give me faith to believe Your promises of healing for my friends who are battling sickness. If You choose to answer in a way besides supernatural healing, remind us to trust in Your love and sovereignty.

Reaching Beyond

☕ **Prayer Focus**–Prayer Warriors

📖 **Scripture Inspiration**

I sought for a man among them who should build up the wall and stand in the breach before me for the land, that I should not destroy it, but I found none. (Ezekiel 22:30 ESV)

🕑 **Praying the Word**

Raise up men and women of prayer who will build a wall of protection and stand before You on behalf of our nation.

🌸 **Prayer Prompt**

Encourage those who tarry with You in prayer. Build their faith, fill them with Your spirit, and give them fresh vision.

☕ **Prayer Focus** _____

📖 Scripture Inspiration

_____

_____

◎ Praying the Word

_____

_____

🌸 Prayer Prompt

_____

_____

_____

☕ **Prayer Focus** _____

📖 Scripture Inspiration

_____

_____

◎ Praying the Word

_____

_____

🌸 Prayer Prompt

_____

_____

_____

Day 18

Praise

☕ **Prayer Focus**—Power

📖 **Scripture Inspiration**

Ah, Lord GOD! It is you who has made the heavens and the earth by your great power and by your outstretched arm! Nothing is too hard for you. (Jeremiah 32:17 ESV)

☺ Praying the Word

I am addressing the Lord God! The One who made the heavens and the earth simply by His great power and outstretched arm. Nothing I bring to You in prayer is beyond Your ability to answer!

✿ Prayer Prompt

I bow before You, aware of my smallness in light of Your greatness. You are awesome and mighty and able to create worlds with a word. I worship You, O powerful God. You are highly exalted, and it is my privilege to offer my simple praise.

🍵 Prayer Focus _____

📖 Scripture Inspiration

_____
_____
_____
_____

⊙ Praying the Word

_____
_____
_____
_____
_____
_____

🌸 Prayer Prompt

_____
_____
_____
_____
_____
_____
_____
_____
_____
_____

173

Day 18
Self

☕ **Prayer Focus**—God's Will

📖 **Scripture Inspiration**

Your ears shall hear a word behind you, saying, "This is the way, walk in it," when you turn to the right or when you turn to the left. (Isaiah 30:21 ESV)

☉ **Praying the Word**

Open my ears so I can hear You directing me which way I should go to find the center of Your will for my life.

🌸 **Prayer Prompt**

You are my Lord, and I submit my will to Yours. I know that it is only in staying within Your plans for my life that I will find the joy and satisfaction of discovering all You created me to be. Help me to discern and find Your will when I don't know which way to turn.

Prayer Focus _____

Scripture Inspiration

_____
_____
_____
_____

Praying the Word

_____
_____
_____
_____
_____
_____

Prayer Prompt

_____
_____
_____
_____
_____
_____
_____
_____
_____
_____

Day 18

Husband

☕ **Prayer Focus**—Peace

📖 **Scripture Inspiration**

Fear not, for I am with you; be not dismayed, for I am your God. I will strengthen you, yes, I will help you. I will uphold you with My righteous right hand. (Isaiah 41:10 NKJV)

☺ **Praying the Word**

Give my husband peace and a strong assurance that You will strengthen him and help him. Remind him not to be worried or afraid because You are not only the God, You are his God, and You will support him as he leans on You.

❀ **Prayer Prompt**

Relieve my husband of any anxiety that he carries with him. Remind him again of Your awesome power and love. Teach him to roll his burdens on to You so that he does not stress under the weight of his responsibilities. Give him sweet sleep and confident assurance that although he may not see how everything is going to work out, You have it all under control.

Prayer Focus _____

Scripture Inspiration

_____

_____

_____

_____

Praying the Word

_____

_____

_____

_____

_____

Prayer Prompt

_____

_____

_____

_____

_____

_____

_____

_____

Day 18
Children

☕ **Prayer Focus**—Diligence

📖 **Scripture Inspiration**

The plans of the diligent lead surely to plenty, but those of everyone who is hasty, surely to poverty. (Proverbs 21:5 NKJV)

☉ Praying the Word

Instruct my children on how to plan ahead and to work diligently so they may enjoy the abundance You desire to heap upon them. Help them to take their time in order to pursue excellence so they don't deprive themselves of Your blessings.

❀ Prayer Prompt

Place within my children a strong work ethic. Give them a healthy pride in their work. Whatever their hands find to do, may they do it with all their might as an offering unto You. Because of their diligence and excellence, may they rise to the top in whatever situation You have them in. Teach them to follow through and care about the details, even if no one else sees but You.

Prayer Focus _____

Scripture Inspiration

_____

_____

_____

_____

Praying the Word

_____

_____

_____

_____

_____

Prayer Prompt

_____

_____

_____

_____

_____

_____

_____

_____

_____

Day 18

Personal Influences

📖 **Scripture Inspiration**

Ask, and it will be given to you; seek, and you will find; knock, and it will be opened to you. (Matthew 7:7 ESV)

🕝 **Praying the Word**

Dear Lord, I'm knocking on the door of heaven, seeking You, and asking You to answer the following requests: _____

🌸 **Prayer Prompt**

Thank You for not being so big that You don't care about every need and for not being too small to answer them all. I lift up these prayer requests and thank You in advance for answering them.

Reaching Beyond

☕ **Prayer Focus**–The Nations

📖 **Scripture Inspiration**

Be still, and know that I am God. I will be exalted among the nations, I will be exalted in the earth! (Psalm 46:10 ESV)

🕝 **Praying the Word**

You are God, and beside You there is no other. Be lifted up so that all nations will worship You.

🌸 **Prayer Prompt**

Almighty God, pour out Your grace, protection, and provision on the homes and families of each person on this planet. May they worship You as their Lord and Creator.

☕ Prayer Focus _____

📖 Scripture Inspiration

_____

_____

☺ Praying the Word

_____

_____

❀ Prayer Prompt

_____

_____

_____

☕ Prayer Focus _____

📖 Scripture Inspiration

_____

_____

☺ Praying the Word

_____

_____

❀ Prayer Prompt

_____

_____

_____

Day 19

Praise

☕ **Prayer Focus**—Hope

📖 **Scripture Inspiration**

May the God of hope fill you with all joy and peace in believing, so that by the power of the Holy Spirit you may abound in hope. (Romans 15:13 ESV)

◎ **Praying the Word**

Dear God of hope, please fill me with all joy and peace. Help me to believe, so that by the power of the Holy Spirit, I may grow ever more full of hope.

🌸 **Prayer Prompt**

My hope is in You, Lord. Even when I have lost hope in the things and people of this world, I am never without hope because I am never without You. Thank You for the plans You have for me, to give me a future and a hope. I will wait expectantly for Your promises to be fulfilled.

Prayer Focus _____

Scripture Inspiration

_____
_____
_____
_____

Praying the Word

_____
_____
_____
_____
_____

Prayer Prompt

_____
_____
_____
_____
_____
_____
_____
_____
_____
_____

Day 19

Self

📖 Scripture Inspiration

But each one is tempted when he is drawn away by his own desires and enticed. Then, when desire has conceived, it gives birth to sin; and sin, when it is full-grown, brings forth death. (James 1:14–15 NKJV)

☺ Praying the Word

Lord, help me to fix my eyes and heart on You and Your Word so that I am so grounded in Truth that I'm not easily drawn away by my own selfish desires and lies from the enemy. Convict me of my unholy thoughts before they have a chance to become sin, which would only bring death to the good and godly plans You have for my life.

❀ Prayer Prompt

I know that temptation isn't a sin, but I want to confess and bring my temptations into Your holy light, because I realize they can easily turn into sin if left in the dark. Please lead me not into temptation and deliver me from the evil one. I desire to do Your will, but I need Your strength when I am weak. Thank You for Your unconditional love.

Prayer Focus _____

Scripture Inspiration

_____

_____

_____

_____

Praying the Word

_____

_____

_____

_____

_____

Prayer Prompt

_____

_____

_____

_____

_____

_____

_____

_____

Day 19

Husband

🍵 **Prayer Focus**—Relationships

📖 Scripture Inspiration

Let us consider how to stir up one another to love and good works, not neglecting to meet together, as is the habit of some, but encouraging one another. (Hebrews 10:24–25 ESV)

☉ Praying the Word

Refresh my husband through godly relationships. Remind him of the importance of meeting regularly with other believers to encourage each other and serve others.

🌸 Prayer Prompt

Strengthen the relationships in my husband's life that are ordained by You. I pray a special bond between my husband and all members of his family. Bring forgiveness, healing, and restoration to any broken relationships. If there is any person in my husband's life who is drawing him away from You, then I ask for an immediate severing of that relationship. Give him godly friendships with men who will encourage him in his walk with You.

🍵 Prayer Focus_____

📖 Scripture Inspiration

_____
_____
_____
_____

🌀 Praying the Word

_____
_____
_____
_____
_____
_____

🌸 Prayer Prompt

_____
_____
_____
_____
_____
_____
_____
_____
_____
_____

Day 19

Children

☕ **Prayer Focus**—Wisdom

📖 **Scripture Inspiration**

When wisdom enters your heart, and knowledge is pleasant to your soul, discretion will preserve you; understanding will keep you, to deliver you from the way of evil. (Proverbs 2:10–12 NKJV)

⊚ **Praying the Word**

Dear Lord, fill my children's heart with Your wisdom. May they experience joy in the pursuit of knowledge. Give them good judgment and common sense to keep them from the paths of the evil one, and deliver them from temptation.

🌸 **Prayer Prompt**

I love the definition that wisdom is supernatural truth lived out in practical ways. Teach my children how to apply the wisdom in Your Word to every situation they encounter in life. I pray that they will walk in the knowledge that You are a practical God and that they would be cheating themselves if they kept You in a "Sunday box." Help me to train them to make asking for wisdom a daily—even moment-by-moment—habit.

🍵 Prayer Focus _____

📖 Scripture Inspiration

_____
_____
_____
_____

🌀 Praying the Word

_____
_____
_____
_____
_____

🌸 Prayer Prompt

_____
_____
_____
_____
_____
_____
_____
_____
_____

Day 19

Personal Influences

☕ **Prayer Focus**–Public Ministries

📖 **Scripture Inspiration**

Now to him who is able to keep you from stumbling and to present you blameless before the presence of his glory with great joy . . . be glory, majesty, dominion, and authority. (Jude 24–25 ESV)

◎ **Praying the Word**

I ask that You keep _____ (public ministry) from stumbling, deliver them from the evil one, and allow them to bring You glory here on earth and eventually in heaven.

🌸 **Prayer Prompt**

I have personally been blessed by this ministry, and I want to offer something in return. So I lift up _____, asking You to pour out the treasures of heaven upon them.

Reaching Beyond

☕ **Prayer Focus**–Other Religions

📖 **Scripture Inspiration**

Jesus said to him, "I am the way, and the truth, and the life. No one comes to the Father except through me." (John 14:6 ESV)

◎ **Praying the Word**

Open everyone's eyes to see that the Way to eternal life with the Father is through the truth of Jesus Christ.

🌸 **Prayer Prompt**

Have mercy on other religions that are looking in the wrong direction for reconciliation with You. Send Your Word and the revelation of the Holy Spirit to bring them to truth.

☕ Prayer Focus _____

📖 Scripture Inspiration

_____

_____

⊙ Praying the Word

_____

_____

✿ Prayer Prompt

_____

_____

_____

☕ Prayer Focus _____

📖 Scripture Inspiration

_____

_____

⊙ Praying the Word

_____

_____

✿ Prayer Prompt

_____

_____

_____

Day 20

Praise

☕ **Prayer Focus**—Coming Again

📖 **Scripture Inspiration**

And if I go and prepare a place for you, I will come again and receive you to Myself; that where I am, there you may be also. (John 14:3 NKJV)

◎ **Praying the Word**

Dear Jesus, You are, even now, preparing a place for me. I cannot wait until You come again and take me unto Yourself. I long to be with You.

❀ **Prayer Prompt**

Even so, come quickly, Lord Jesus! The promise of Your sure return is almost more than I can even fathom. Thank You that this world is not all that life is about. I am grateful for the gift of life, but even more so for the gift of eternal life with You! Help me to prepare for You and be ready when You come to take me as Your bride. I love You.

Prayer Focus_____

📖 Scripture Inspiration

_____
_____
_____
_____

☺ Praying the Word

_____
_____
_____
_____
_____
_____

🦋 Prayer Prompt

_____
_____
_____
_____
_____
_____
_____
_____
_____

Day 20

Self

☕ **Prayer Focus**—Finances

📖 Scripture Inspiration

If you are untrustworthy about worldly wealth, who will trust you with the true riches of heaven? (Luke 16:11 NLT)

☺ Praying the Word

I want You to be able to trust me with all that You have given us here on earth so You can depend on me for the really valuable blessings that are eternal.

❀ Prayer Prompt

First of all, thank You for supplying all our needs. My heart is to have a spirit of gratitude rather than the temptation to focus on wanting things I don't have. Provide all the resources we need to be able to pay our bills, and keep us from the temptation to go into debt. Give me discernment for how to be wise in spending and creative in saving.

🍵 Prayer Focus_____

📖 Scripture Inspiration

_____

_____

_____

_____

⑨ Praying the Word

_____

_____

_____

_____

_____

_____

🦋 Prayer Prompt

_____

_____

_____

_____

_____

_____

_____

_____

_____

_____

Day 20
Husband

☕ **Prayer Focus**—Love

📖 **Scripture Inspiration**

You shall love the Lord your God with all your heart and with all your soul and with all your strength and with all your mind, and your neighbor as yourself. (Luke 10:27 ESV)

☺ Praying the Word

May my husband be so assured of Your love for him that his heart, soul, mind, and strength overflow with love for You and others.

✤ Prayer Prompt

Thank You, Jesus, that we can love You because You first loved us. Open my husband's heart to receive the fullness of that love and bask in it. Reveal a new facet of Your loveliness to him every day, so much so that he falls in love with You over and over again. Teach him how to give that love away to others.

☕ Prayer Focus _____

📖 Scripture Inspiration

_____
_____
_____
_____

🌀 Praying the Word

_____
_____
_____
_____
_____
_____

🌸 Prayer Prompt

_____
_____
_____
_____
_____
_____
_____
_____
_____

Day 20
Children

☕ **Prayer Focus**—Forgiveness

📖 **Scripture Inspiration**

The discretion of a man makes him slow to anger, and his glory is to overlook a transgression. (Proverbs 19:11 NKJV)

☉ **Praying the Word**

Help my children to see the wisdom in not responding in the heat of the moment. May they reflect Your glory and overlook the faults of others just as You have overlooked their own sins.

🌼 **Prayer Prompt**

Jesus, I pray that my children will walk freely in Your forgiveness and then extend that mercy to those around them. Help them to be quick to forgive those who have hurt them and to release them from any need to pay for the pain they have caused. Help my children to realize that forgiving someone doesn't make the other person right, but it does set their own heart free from any bitterness that could take root and choke the abundant life from them.

🍵 Prayer Focus_____

📖 Scripture Inspiration

_____

_____

_____

_____

⊙ Praying the Word

_____

_____

_____

_____

_____

_____

🌸 Prayer Prompt

_____

_____

_____

_____

_____

_____

_____

_____

_____

_____

Day 20

Personal Influences

☕ **Prayer Focus**–Favorite Authors/Ministers

📖 **Scripture Inspiration**
Commit your work to the LORD, and your plans will be established.
(Proverbs 16:3 ESV)

☉ **Praying the Word**
Lord, remind my favorite author/minister, _____, to
hand over any dreams and desires into Your care so Your plans
may be fulfilled for Your ministry.

❀ **Prayer Prompt**
I pray that You will bless and multiply the ministry of _____
so that many other lives will be touched. As You expand his/her
influence, draw him/her closer to Your heart.

Reaching Beyond

☕ **Prayer Focus**–The Body of Christ

📖 **Scripture Inspiration**
*We, though many, are one body in Christ, and individually mem-
bers one of another.* (Romans 12:5 ESV)

☉ **Praying the Word**
With You as our Head, I ask You to knit us together as one body
so that we may work as a team to reveal Your glory.

❀ **Prayer Prompt**
Purify and strengthen the body of Christ to walk in unity and
grace. Tear down walls and build bridges between us. Teach us
how to edify one another and build each other up.

Prayer Focus _____

Scripture Inspiration

_____

_____

Praying the Word

_____

_____

Prayer Prompt

_____

_____

_____

Prayer Focus _____

Scripture Inspiration

_____

_____

Praying the Word

_____

_____

Prayer Prompt

_____

_____

_____

THE **M**♥**therhood**CLUB ™

Making a Difference One Kiss at a Time

mc

...born from a simple idea: *honor Mom for doing
the most important job in the world.*

Titles included in THE **M**♥**therhood**CLUB™:

Prayer Guide: *The Busy Mom's Guide to Prayer*
—Lisa Whelchel

Parenting: *Mom-PhD*
—Teresa Bell Kindred

There's a Perfect Little Angel in Every Child
—Gigi Schweikert

Inspiration: *The Miracle in a Mother's Hug*
—Helen Burns

Gift: *Holding the World by the Hand*
—Gigi Schweikert

Fiction: *Tight Squeeze*
—Debbie DiGiovanni

Devotional: *"I'm a Good Mother"*
—Gigi Schweikert

"At the Motherhood
Club, you'll find books
to meet all your
mothering needs."
—Lisa Whelchel
(From *The Facts of Life*)